THE WORLD AND U2

THE WORLD AND U2

One Band's Remaking of Global Activism

Alan McPherson

ROWMAN & LITTLEFIELD
Lanham • Boulder • New York • London

Published by Rowman & Littlefield
A wholly owned subsidiary of The Rowman & Littlefield Publishing Group, Inc.
4501 Forbes Boulevard, Suite 200, Lanham, Maryland 20706
www.rowman.com

Unit A, Whitacre Mews, 26-34 Stannary Street, London SE11 4AB

British Library Cataloguing in Publication Information Available

Library of Congress Cataloging-in-Publication Data

McPherson, Alan L.
The world and U2 : one band's remaking of global activism / Alan McPherson.
p. cm.
Includes bibliographical references and index.
ISBN 978-1-4422-4933-2 (cloth : alk. paper) – ISBN 978-1-4422-4934-9 (ebook)
1. U2 (Musical group) 2. Bono, 1960– Political activity. 3. Edge (Musician), 1961– Political activity.
4. Rock musicians–Political activity. I. Title.
ML421.U2M37 2015
782.42166092'2–dc23
[B] 2015002421

∞ ™ The paper used in this publication meets the minimum requirements of American National Standard for Information Sciences Permanence of Paper for Printed Library Materials, ANSI/NISO Z39.48-1992.

Printed in the United States of America

A12006654979

To my brother Ian,
who taught me to play and love music

CONTENTS

LIST OF FIGURES

ACKNOWLEDGMENTS

Thanks first of all to Brian Betteridge for fact-checking the entire book against his encyclopedic knowledge of U2 and thus saving me from embarrassing mistakes. Also helpful was everyone at atu2.com, by far the best unofficial website and an incredible archive about the band. The work of Scott Calhoun and Matt McGee deserves special praise. At the University of Oklahoma, graduate students Joe Hartmann and Jeffrey Swanson helped me figure out the outer limits of the universe of U2 publications. Deans Zach Messitte and Suzette Grillot allowed me to pursue this unorthodox line of research. The College of International Studies provided funding for the index and photographs. Heather Dubnick did a great job with the index. My wife, Cindy, was enthusiastic about the project all along. And my sons, Luc and Nico, who know nothing about U2, were a welcome distraction and a reminder of why I care about activism.

INTRODUCTION

U2 in a Selfish World

We're just trying to figure out how to live in this world.—The Edge[1]

Ever since I became a fan of U2, I have been trying to reach them. My first encounter with singer Bono, guitarist The Edge, drummer Larry Mullen Jr., and bassist Adam Clayton came in the summer of 1984, when a friend played me a vinyl record of their then-new live EP *Under a Blood Red Sky*.

An idealistic but hormonal 13-year-old, I was looking to diversify my tastes beyond the heavy metal that dominated my outlook that year. U2 offered loud, guitar-driven rock but without the hypermasculinity, breakneck speed, or ludicrous devil worship of 1980s metal.[2] U2 also appeared to care about something, though I wasn't sure what yet.

I attended their show at the Montreal Forum in 1985 and was hooked. Like many fans, I liked their records just fine, but the live experience was something else altogether. Its feeling of social consciousness, community, and transcendence proved more powerful than any church had ever filled me with. I was close enough to the stage to get the exhilarating sensation that Bono was actually looking at me as he swayed precariously on top of a speaker stack. His every word and act seemed wise beyond his years, and he was only in his mid-twenties.

In those pre-Internet days, I combed record stores in search of every U2 album, single, and rare import and bootleg. In 1987, now at the Olympic Stadium show in Montreal, I made it to the edge of the stage when Bono picked the person next to me to play his guitar on "People Get Ready" because he had injured his shoulder. U2 remained beyond my reach.

In the quarter century that followed *The Joshua Tree*, I attended four more U2 shows, remaining dedicated and hoping to meet the band. After my first missed opportunity in Montreal, a second came in Paris when friends at a youth hostel invited me to an all-night dance club. I was jetlagged and declined. I learned the following day that The Edge and Larry had been there, chatting up fellow clubgoers. I kicked myself again.

Luckily for me, I didn't love my favorite band in self-righteous isolation. All the teenagers I knew, it seemed, loved U2 or at least respected them. Girls loved U2, which mattered a lot. Their music played at every party, blared from every car stereo. Even the 1960s generation, to which my parents belonged, liked the band. *Rolling Stone*, a magazine by and for baby boomers, in its desperation to find young bands to celebrate, prematurely crowned U2 the "Band of the Eighties" in 1985. Two years later, *Time* put them on the cover—only the third rock band so honored.[3]

U2 were at once a band for their times and a true original. Their sound, reflecting the democracy inside the band, made space for all four members, yet the chiming, soaring notes of guitarist The Edge marked the 1980s and spawned countless imitators. U2 was the sound track of earnestness and hope in a bleak decade marked by the false optimism of Ronald Reagan.

To be sure, in my efforts to connect with the band, I was not beyond finding fault in them. Over time, the repetitiveness of Bono's live behavior—plucking fans from the audience and making political speeches—dissipated some of the magic from my first encounter with them back in Montreal. And I've found a few albums and more than a few songs to be unambitious or uninspired.

But, like many fans, I have stuck with them because of their desire to innovate musically and perhaps more because of their personalities. Bono's sincerity, his desire to connect with each and every soul in the audience, never seemed in doubt. Like the Beatles, U2 owed part of their success to their charisma and specifically their sense of humor.[4] I was always dumbfounded in the 1980s when Bono refused to transport his charming live self onto the mainstream media, where instead he appeared, like the rest of the band, grim faced and self-important in often black-and-white photography.

Still, from the late 1980s on, the world embraced U2 as the biggest band in the world. In their now nearly 40-year career, U2 has sold about 150 million albums and 30 million tickets to its shows and won 22 Grammy awards. Their 2014 album, *Songs of Innocence*, which Apple released for free to the 500 million users of its iTunes software, was listened to in part at least 80 million times in its first weeks.[5] The band won countless other artistic awards and appeared on just about every conceivable magazine cover and radio and television talk show. "It is arguable that, mind for mind, heart for heart, the impact of U2 in both the US and the rest of the western world is now at the very least comparable to that of the Beatles," wrote Irish writer John Waters back in 1994.[6]

In the 1990s and 2000s, I grew up, diversified my tastes some more, and lost the intense passion for the band I had in my youth. I had never met them and probably never would and became an academic studying "serious" issues.

* * *

But a few years ago, I realized that I could reconnect with Bono and the band by writing about something we should all take seriously—their activism. I recalled that if it was not U2 that introduced me to issues such as war, poverty, human rights, religious strife, and other key issues—I owe that to great literature and fine teachers—it was that faraway, so-close Irish band that made it seem cool to care about those same issues.

The evidence of U2's effectiveness as global activists is overwhelming. Most who have written about their work would agree with author Greg Garrett, who called Bono "in many ways, the most important activist in the world."[7] Journalist James Traub found him "the most politically effective figure in the recent history of popular culture."[8] Bono has helped wring tens of billions of dollars for the poor out of the U.S. political system and tens of billions more from other developed nations. His pleas for help have reached billions through live concerts, radio, television, and the Internet. U2's philanthropy also proved enduring. They played their first benefit concert in 1978 for the Contraception Action Campaign. In 2015, one website specializing in celebrity charity calculated that U2 was involved in 22 charities and 22 causes, while Bono supported 38 charities and 28 causes, making him the site's fifth "top celebrity."[9] By that same year, (RED), a part of Bono's ONE organization, had raised over $300 million to fight HIV/AIDS.

Why was it U2 and not another band that became global activists? Why was Bono, a musician, more effective than anybody else at changing minds and raising funds? What sustained the band through decades of work on behalf of the world's most vulnerable, and how did those efforts change during those decades? Perhaps most important, how did U2 contribute to a new kind of global activism led by celebrities?

U2 did not single-handedly "remake" global activism. But it has stood at the vanguard of new trends and strategies in activism since the early 1980s. Equally important, U2's remaking of the world of global activism should be understood as a reaction to their times.

The times that U2 have lived through as teens and adults so far—the 1970s to the 2010s—were marked by a global political economy responding primarily to the selfish impulses of the wealthiest and the most powerful. To be sure, self-interest is universal, and egoism did not spring up suddenly in the 1970s.[10] But, in that decade and since, governments around the world, from London to Beijing, largely gave up mid-century dreams of distributing fairly economic resources, sustaining workers' rights, and building and maintaining large public goods, such as highways and hospitals. Instead, they produced political systems, taxation schemes, and public policies by and for the rich that left behind the very notion of public good. Those policies included lifting regulations so that transnational corporations could destroy the planet more quickly, attack unions, endanger workers, pay fewer (or no) taxes, and increase profits to ludicrous heights.[11] Many economies entered a postindustrial phase characterized by low-paid services replacing manufacturing and by the hijacking of economies by financial speculators on Wall Street and elsewhere. Market triumphalism meant the privatization of almost every formerly government-run service, from health care to education to defense.[12]

The cynicism of the rich trickled down to most of the middle class and the poor, who stopped expecting altruism or honesty from their leaders. Thus, philosopher Elena Pulcini has identified a "global Self" emerging from late twentieth-century globalization. This person typically suffers from a "pathology" of "unlimited individualism" that afflicts equally the parasitic consumer, the indifferent spectator, and the narcissistic creator. All suffer an "erosion of the social bond." While the individual has for centuries been assumed to be the rational subject at the heart of society, the global age has created in the individual

> a subjectivity . . . clinging to the immediacy of the present and fleeting pleasures, the unconscious victim of rampant conformism, with a parasitic relationship with a world that has been reduced to an immense factory of goods, prey to fears and insecurity and inclined towards entropy. At the same time, it is a subjectivity driven by a vocation towards the unlimited expansion of selfish desires and expectations, making it blind to the desires and requirements of others. [13]

Many others, from Christopher Lasch to Charles Taylor, have commented for decades on the prevalence of narcissism in our modern societies. [14] This obsession with one's own desires, egged on by consumer capitalism, makes the modern individual acquisitive, passive, and easily manipulated as society meanwhile becomes increasingly fragmented and atomized. [15] Researchers have now confirmed a sharp rise in narcissism: from the early 1970s to 2013, the proportion of young American adults saying that "being very well off financially" was an important life goal climbed from about 45 to 82 percent. And the young were more likely to be narcissistic: in 2008, 9.4 of Americans in their twenties had experienced narcissistic personality disorder, which afflicted only 3.2 percent of those over 65. From plastic surgery to naming patterns to social networking, every indicator pointed to an increasingly unhealthy self-obsession. By the 2000s, too, China and the rest of the world were "starting to follow America's lead." [16] One logical outcome was a society-wide retreat from activism, arising out of what Robert Putnam identified as declining "social capital." [17]

Other clear results of selfishness were a yawning income gap and broader social inequality in many countries. Again, the United States led the pack. In 1970, the top 10 percent of U.S. earners made 32 percent of the income; by 2012, their share was over 50 percent. From 1970 to 2007, the top 0.01 percent's share went up from 0.7 to over 6 percent. Meanwhile, the poverty rate moved up, and family incomes fell. The United Kingdom lived through a similar trend, as did Canada, Australia, New Zealand, and Ireland, all since the 1970s. In India, too, the top brackets since the 1980s were back to their dominance from the 1920s and 1930s. Argentina, meanwhile, saw its inequality increase as of the 1990s. Even the most egalitarian countries in the world—Sweden, Finland, and Norway—saw their inequality reach as high or higher than the previous 40 years. Israel, Japan, Russia, Hungary, the Czech Republic, and China—anywhere one looked, the story was the same.[18]

Inequality between rich and poor nations also increased, again since the 1970s. Up to about 1978, the so-called third world grew its economy relatively quickly.[19] But from the late 1970s on, the leaders of the world economy struck back. While global per capita income tripled between 1960 and the mid-1990s, over 100 countries saw their income decline since the 1980s.[20] And inequality was a basic factor in the problems of the world. As development expert Dan Brockington wrote in 2014, "The key problem that development and humanitarian organisations address . . . is the problem of inequality."[21]

Some changes were not due strictly to selfishness. Oil shocks increased production costs everywhere and made economies less productive, and the United States faced competition from rising powers, such as Japan and Germany, and stopped being a capital exporter to developing countries, which also raised interest rates on loans that those countries had taken out.

But the rich also rewrote the "rules of the game" at institutions such as the International Monetary Fund and the World Trade Organization. They made easier and cheaper the export of manufactured goods from multinational corporations while limiting laborers' movement across borders and hiking subsidies on the West's agricultural exports, devastating the largely agricultural developing world and institutionalized "anti-poor biases in the international rules."[22] To make things worse, poor countries, such as India, or previously poor countries, such as China, argued that it was their turn to be selfish, that they could pollute as much as they wanted in their quest to catch up to the developed world.

Politics changed, too. In these same 40 years or so, political leaders around the world seemed increasingly beholden to lobbyists and donors who evinced no belief in the common good and instead served the exclusive interests of the wealthy global elite.

The end of the Cold War in the early 1990s was supposed to enhance democracy and fairness. The East–West confrontation ruled global politics until the 1990s, accounting for much of the human rights abuses that U2 denounced, as in Poland and Central America. But its dissipation, rather than lead to greater peace and democracy, allowed for ethnic and religious strife and good old-fashioned land hunger to return to the fore, as in Bosnia, Burma, and Russia. There were, of course, partial exceptions, such as South Africa, where apartheid died a well-deserved death. But the selfishness of economic elites failed to get the country ready to face a new pandemic—of HIV/AIDS this time. The dissolving of Cold War ideologies seemed to convince many that idealism had been a destructive force and that the pursuit of pragmatic self-interest was fully justified.

The triumph of liberal capitalism over communism also let loose a particularly savage individualism, not to mention a heightened competition within and between countries.[23] Globalization was partly to blame. Although some of its impact was welcome, globalization increased selfishness in two ways. First, the communications revolution allowed the more talented, better educated, luckier, and especially the already wealthier among us to reach a worldwide audience, and thus in every profession emerged a "star system" that rewarded a few with extravagant salaries and bonuses while the many suffered a loss in purchasing power.[24] Second, the increased circulation of people diversified the ethnic background of populations, especially in the global North. The response by those already there was often to exclude newcomers—called "illegals" or "refugees" or just plain immigrants—by erecting barriers to citizenship, political participation, or equality.[25]

As a result of these broad changes, legislators grew cynical about political processes and merely pushed through more laws to help the already powerful without heeding the clear wishes of the electorate.[26] Throughout the globe, citizens hoping for greater political opportunity and equality saw the rise of "illiberal democracies" and plutocracies, or governments by and for the rich. In Western so-called democracies, conservatives disguised their schemes to wrench public services from the poor and concentrate private property into fewer hands as fiscal responsibility or a "cultural war" against the excesses of the liberal welfare state that supposedly redistributed the wealth of the deserving to the lazy, the mentally deficient, or the drug addled. Economist John Kenneth Galbraith saw through their charade. "The modern conservative," he observed, "is engaged in one of man's oldest exercises in moral philosophy; that is, the search for a superior moral justification for selfishness."[27]

U2 came on the scene as a countercurrent to this selfishness. From one of the poorest nations in the developed world, these four young men refused to wallow in either the cynicism of the right or the nihilism of the left and of youth culture. They identified the remnants of altruism in Western societies and exhorted them, concert after concert, cause after cause, to fight their selfish reflexes.

It could be plausibly argued that today, thanks to Bono more than to any other individual, caring for the most vulnerable people on the planet has become an integral part of international relations as embodied in summits, treaties, and the like. Selfishness still makes the wheels turn, to be sure, but the world has become considerably less selfish because of U2's engagement with it. As Scott Calhoun writes, "U2's fans know that things have changed for the better because of U2."[28]

* * *

This book contributes historical context to U2's activism, adding to a vibrant "U2 studies" literature that has produced not only dozens of books and articles but also dissertations, theses, a journal, and even academic conferences.[29] That nonmusic literature, however, has targeted religious audiences,[30] academics and musicologists,[31] and even young adults and the business reader.[32] U2's activism is still in need of its own book.[33]

As chapter 1 explains, U2 emerged out of late 1970s Ireland as a result of a combination of factors—post-1960s disillusionment not only with traditional authority but also with the counterculture, poverty and joblessness, and violent religious strife in Northern Ireland and sometimes in Ireland itself. Before 1982, the band was focused far more on "making it" than on changing the world, but the influences on its activism were taking root.

Chapter 2 surveys the 1980s, arguing that the band's activism bloomed as U2 tackled famine, the imprisonment of prisoners of conscience, and apartheid, among other causes, all while branding itself a "band that cares." But U2's 1980s were also largely limited to consciousness raising and fund-raising.

Chapter 3 observes a paradox: as U2's public image became more removed from activism in the 1990s, the band members actually graduated from consciousness raising to direct action, from talking about causes to doing something about them. Their involvement with Greenpeace, Bosnian war victims, and the Good Friday Agreement illustrated their deepening commitment.

Chapter 4 takes on the all-important early 2000s, when Bono made the jump from activist on the outside of the system to lobbyist trying from the inside to effect meaningful, large-scale change through legislation. The success he enjoyed and the strategies he employed were unprecedented. They demonstrated his unique ability to awaken the best instincts out of the most powerful (and often the most selfish) people in the world, such as legislators and social conservatives, who made up two new constituencies for U2.

Where most treatments of Bono's activism were written in the mid-2000s, chapter 5 updates the story to 2015. It introduces new elements, one being Bono's transformation of his potentially fleeting celebrity diplomacy into a network of permanent philanthropic and lobbying groups that ensconced Bono more than ever into traditional establishment circles. The danger inherent in such traditionalism was that Bono, by spending so much time with the rich, would absorb their worldview and forget about the poor—the second element. As the band's and especially Bono's wealth skyrocketed in the 2000s, U2 drew accusations of hypocrisy for both its activism and its business practices. While few criticisms proved substantive, they did show that Bono adjusted his worldview both to satisfy the egos of the rich from whom he was demanding enormous contributions and to respond to critics who questioned the very practice of sending aid to poor countries. Bono could neither fundamentally change the economic system nor permanently move the hearts of the most powerful, but his efforts nevertheless left a lasting imprint.

* * *

Crosscutting this narrative are three themes that help explain the unique success of U2's philanthropy and that, it is hoped, offer lessons to activists.[34] These "secrets to success" usually combine one of U2's core beliefs with an effective method, a way of "being in the world," as The Edge notes in the epigraph. More important, these are lessons from U2's life that all activists or would-be activists should carry with them as they fight injustice.

First among these lessons is the band's grounding in their *community*. By that, I do mean—to a point—their Irishness: the young men who formed a band in 1976 were uniquely exposed to near–developing world conditions while living on the margins of the developed world in a free market economy in which anyone of great talent could become rich and famous. Unlike, say, Quebecers or Basques, both of whom also experienced terrorism in the 1970s, the Irish spoke English and could thus reach global audiences with the most common vernacular in the world of rock and roll. When U2 played at the famed Slane Castle in 2001, Bono said of his Irish audience, "This is our tribe."[35]

Yet U2's Irishness was always ambivalent. "I grew up at points with the sense that what was Irish was a bit crap," Bono once said.[36] Many Irish have returned the favor, refusing to be proud of U2 as an export. One scholar complained that too few have written about U2's Irishness, which is true but also explained by the fact that U2 have never defined their sense of place only or even principally by their nationality.[37]

U2 are in fact Dubliners before they are Irishmen. The tight-knit group that composed the U2 community almost all came from that city, and many have remained there. All U2 band members keep a home there. They have invested there, and they have largely recorded there. At the height of his *Joshua Tree*–era superstardom, Bono explained that "Dublin is our anchor, I suppose. You get so high sometimes when you are on stage and you need to come down, and you really do that in Dublin. The people here don't allow you to act like a rock star. It's a reminder of how important our family and friends are, how very much we need them to keep us from being swallowed up in the pop world. . . . I want to hold on to who I am."[38] U2 still hold on to each other even when not in Ireland. Bono and The Edge own condominiums close to each other in the south of France. Their spouses and children often join them on tour.[39] The larger touring community of U2 has also been tight-knit. Joe O'Herlihy, U2's chief sound engineer, and designer Stave Averill continue to work with the band after more than three decades.[40] Manager Paul McGuinness, the unofficial fifth member of the band since its infancy, retired only in 2013. What did this teach Bono? "People with a strong sense of family and community . . . are always very strong people."[41]

U2 have long lived the tension between their communal, isolated origins and the globe that they quite literally inhabit today. One of Bono's fiercest Irish critics backhandedly complimented him for being "nothing if not cosmopolitan" and "the most thoroughly transatlantic of elite figures."[42] To many philosophers, by contrast, cosmopolitanism has a positive ring. It connotes not only the recognition of differences among the peoples of the globe but also their interconnecting commonalities. Cosmopolitanism embraces the struggle for a universal moral order—a U2 precept if there ever was one. A global citizen thus is self-aware, open minded, accepting of different cultures, and thirsty for knowledge and human community.[43] As Kwame Appiah notes, cosmopolitanism is not a newfangled concept but dates back to the Cynics of the fourth century BCE who envisioned "citizens of the cosmos." It long entailed that all of us have obligations toward people we do not know—the essence of an unselfish person. In an era of intense globalization, cosmopolitans underscore ethical and humanitarian aspects of life that run against the instinct toward selfishness.[44]

"Not wanting to go home, but wanting a home to go home to, is a dark deep undercurrent of U2's loud, sad songs," writer John Waters noted.[45] Adam, the least Irish of the four, agreed: "I'm beginning to feel more in common with those people out there who are exiles, who can't come back . . . you're even questioning how important your role in domestic Ireland is. Or whether there is a wider world out there you can contribute to."[46] Bono also admitted to rootlessness. In the late 1980s, he described himself "as someone who does not know who he is. . . . When I was growing up . . . I didn't know if I was middle class, working class, Catholic, Protestant. . . . I never actually thought about it."[47]

Through the years, the band did think about the tension between community and cosmopolitanism, and the voyage, painful but fruitful, has informed their activism as much as their music. The *Joshua Tree-Rattle and Hum* period was their most notable effort to grow roots. U2 discovered a part of themselves through America: "There is something Irish about the subject of oppression. . . . So you see we found the 'Irish Thing' through the American: Gospel, Blues, Robert Johnson, Bob Dylan, these became passports home."[48] In the 1990s, U2 followed a more chaotic but still rewarding quest through European identity, one that helped the band come to terms with its increasing globality. By 1998, Bono admitted that "I feel a bit more comfortable about not knowing who I am."[49] Waters argued cogently that, as members of a postcolonial society, it was this search for identity that allowed U2 to create such open music, sonically and lyrically, that connected to the rest of the world. "They have realized that being Irish gives them the ultimate freedom to be anything. There are no rules, no codes, by which they have to live."[50]

This struggle for self-definition drew many fans to U2 and also shaped Bono as an activist. As one author wrote that Bono "models for fans of

U2 the complexities, pitfalls, and potential triumphs of constructing an 'authentic self' in a world fraught with tricky 'post'-paradigms: postnationalism, poststructuralism, postcolonialism. . . . He succeeds in constructing a model of ethical and artistic engagement."[51] For instance, being Irish has informed Bono's consistent rejection of violence in struggles for justice: "I am an Irishman and we are an Irish group . . . but I'm frightened of borders, frightened of restrictions on those levels and I get scared when people start saying they're prepared to kill to back their belief."[52]

A second major lesson that runs through U2's global activism is *faith*. Values inherited from their Christian beliefs and enriched through study and observation built a foundation of humanistic values far more solid in U2 than in other major Western pop artists. Their anger at injustice mirrored Jesus's outrage, yet none of the members belonged to a church or to any organized religion after the early 1980s. All four grew up in an Ireland where religion was losing its overwhelming influence, and so they faced the rest of the world with a skeptical but still hopeful gaze. Because of their own conflicting feelings about organized religion, U2 were often driven to aim for religious ecstasy during their concerts. Bono often asked the audience, "Have you ever been to church?," only to add, "*This* is church!"[53]

Bono's view of how selfish religion had become long expressed itself in seething wrath. "To me, we are living in the most unchristian times," he told *Rolling Stone* in 1987. "When I see these racketeers, the snake oil salesmen on these right wing television stations, asking for not your $20 or your $50 but your $100 in the name of Jesus Christ, I just want to throw up." In Ireland, he added, "they force feed you religion. . . . It's about control: birth control, control over marriage. This has nothing to do with liberation."[54]

U2's faith-informed music clearly shored up believers among their fans. "U2's music let me know I was not alone and that there was something more than just darkness, if I could only hang on," recounted author Greg Garrett. "U2's music is attempting to do more than chronicle sexual conquests and incite rebellion, rock 'n' roll's traditional subject matter. . . . Life is not about acquisition or conquest nor is it about just saving yourself for an afterlife. . . . U2 models for us the idea of spiritual journey, rather than that of reaching a spiritual destination."[55]

As the globe's problems grew in seriousness, Christians looked increasingly to U2 for inspiration. Writing in 2003, one vicar noted that "the extent of human impact can be seen too clearly: a row of oil wells flaming in Saudi Arabia, oil slicks in the Arabian Sea, and deforestation in the Amazon. . . . Today, the fears are not so much around nuclear attack but around the far more ordinary things that can so easily be turned into weapons of war: airplanes, postal systems, drinking water, dirty bombs, smallpox. . . . And it is all too easy to imagine that God has abandoned us."[56]

U2's faith reinforced its sense of community in that it helped the four band members stay together through what is approaching four decades—the only popular band to have lasted so long intact. Adam, also the least religious of the bunch, admitted that "a certain amount of [U2's unity], I suppose, could be called Christian principles: not wishing to sell your brother down the river, believing in your viewpoint." He also explicitly ascribed the band's cohesiveness to nationality: "I think very much that that is an Irish thing. . . . I think it's very much, when you come from this island, there is a natural instinct to stick together outside of it."[57]

U2's faith also explicitly teaches the third lesson of this book—*action*, or the transformation of belief into pragmatic steps intended to bring about change. "If we want to live a rich and interesting (not to mention holy) life," continued Garrett, U2 "tell us it should be a compassionate and useful life, a life devoted to peace and justice. We are called to carry each other, not because it is easy, but because it is right, and we are called to elevation, not purely for ourselves, but for one another."[58] One theologian heard in U2 "a prophetic voice. . . . Amos crafted poems, Jeremiah wept sermons, Isaiah alternately rebuked and comforted, Ezekiel did street theater. U2 writes songs and goes on tour, singing them." In so doing, the band "challenge the people of God to live 'in accordance with the scriptures,' scriptures that are especially vocal about care for the poor, the suffering, and the disreputable."[59] Bono himself often reiterated the message of liberation theology "that God is with the vulnerable and the poor. God is in the slums, in the cardboard boxes where the poor play house. God is in the silence of a mother who has infected her child with a virus that will end both their lives. God is in the cries heard under the rubble of war."[60] A minister saw in Bono and U2 "a wonderful example of what it means to *live by grace*. We desperately need such examples, because in our contemporary US culture, grace has become nearly incomprehensible."[61]

As this book demonstrates, U2 and especially Bono transformed from idealists who denounced policies or advocated for new ones into pragmatists who still hold on to ideals dearly but are willing to do the grunt work and to compromise in order to achieve realistic ends. As late as 2013, Bono admitted learning from 1960s icons Bob Dylan, John Lennon, and Bob Marley that "the world outside the window was not fixed. It was more malleable than everyone else was telling you." Yet he discarded the "dreaming" of the 1960s in favor of the "doing" of the twenty-first century.[62]

His bandmates agreed with their leader's newfound determination. Adam saw in Bono's political work a win-win situation for the world and the band: "People see and hear a very pragmatic, determined man, who is not in it for the glamour, who is getting up early, going to those meetings, having those arguments and slowly gaining ground. It is a real job, and he is getting results. . . . He is very realistic and humble, in terms of going after these things. And when he comes back to the band, . . . it's fun. He can cut loose."[63]

Larry, as always, was more succinct: Bono would "have lunch with the devil himself if it gets him what he needs."[64]

* * *

Community, *faith*, and *action*: such are the lessons—the pillars—of U2's activism. They have run through every period of their lives, even if at times they were lying in wait or explicitly hidden from the press. In later decades, all three lessons became explicit and allowed four teenagers from Ireland to feel confident that their values and good works rested on sound moral foundations.

These lessons should not be those only of spoiled rock stars, as Bono is fond of calling himself. They could and should be identified by all as tools that allow activists to identify their supporters, commit to values, and achieve their goals. If handled with care, community, faith, and action should allow all of us to "reach" U2.

I

OUT OF IRELAND, 1960–1982

The worst things in the world are justified by belief.—Bono and The Edge, "Raised by Wolves"

The crises rocking Ireland—and more broadly the West—in the 1970s shaped the childhoods, meeting, and first years as a band of the members of U2. The "Me Decade" signified the end of the idealist 1960s, but it was a misnomer. It ushered in *several* decades of "me"-oriented social trends and government policies that made cynicism and selfishness the new norms and set U2 on the path of global activism.

The four young men who were to form U2—Adam Clayton, Dave Evans, Paul Hewson, and Larry Mullen (Mullen added the "Jr." after he became famous to clear up confusion with his father)—grew up just as those new norms overlapped with the sectarian divide between Protestants and Catholics in Northern Ireland, which, starting in the late 1960s, erupted into a period of political violence known as The Troubles. Living in the Irish capital of Dublin, the four were never directly exposed to the terrorism in the North. Yet the poverty, joblessness, street violence, religious conservatism, and other problems in Ireland drove U2 to challenge conventions in this deeply conventional society. Unique among Irish musicians, they sought success beyond the United Kingdom. Their early contributions to music and activism—sensitive, defiant, universal, yet firmly grounded in Irishness—reflected the mix of ambition and worldliness that would characterize their later blossoming into global activists.

The four boys of U2 were born between March 1960 and October 1961. In an Ireland rent by religious strife, Adam, Dave, Paul, and Larry,

Figure 1.1. **U2 before they were activists. Dave "The Edge" Evans, Paul "Bono" Hewson, Adam Clayton, and Larry Mullen Jr. in their tour van, Leeds, United Kingdom, 1976.** *Martyn Goddard/REX USA*

while not outlandishly deviant, stood out for their ecumenical origins. At mid-century, only 125,000 Protestants lived in an Ireland of 3 million. David Evans's parents were two of them and, to boot, were of Welsh origin and had migrated from England. As a result, young David felt like "a freak, and I spent a few years where I was pretty quiet. I didn't go out an awful lot. Those were the years when I listened to the most music."[1] Adam was also from England, and his father flew for the Royal Air Force.

Paul's parents, meanwhile, engaged in a rare mixed marriage. His Catholic father, Bob, defied Church practice—which called for special dispensation by Rome, bringing up children Catholic, and holding the ceremony in a darkened church—by marrying Iris Rankin in a church of her own Protestant faith in 1950. Only years later would a Catholic priest bless their union.[2]

And only a decade after their sacrilegious wedding would Paul be born. "I always felt like I was sitting on the fence," he later recalled about his mixed-faith family.[3] He and his older brother, Norman, were raised Protestant while his father continued to attend Mass by himself. Paul hated this religious segregation.[4]

U2's later activism may have also stemmed from teenage family traumas. When Paul was 14, his mother, Iris, died suddenly of a cerebral aneurysm at her own father's funeral. Larry's mother followed, the victim of a fatal traffic accident when he was 17. Teenage parental loss placed the two in the company of John Lennon, Paul McCartney, Jimi Hendrix, and Madonna, pop stars who forever sought to regain their mothers' affection through fame.[5] On the liner notes or "flashbacks" of *Songs of Innocence* (2014), an album dedicated to memories from Ireland and Dublin in the 1970s, Bono recalls "beautiful Iris, humour as black as her curls . . . practical and magical. . . . I owe Iris. Her absence, I filled with music. [A]fter grief comes rage . . . the molten lava that turns to rock if it can."

In the Hewson household, Iris had been kind and sensitive and Paul's only champion. His father, while fundamentally a romantic and a lover of music, was too harsh and stuck in traditional masculine ways to fulfill his son's needs. Bono later reflected that his creativity may have been a reflex against a father who was "deeply cynical about the world and the characters in it" and advised his son "never to dream." His mother's absence left a deep hole. "I felt a real resentment, because I actually had never got a chance . . . to feel that unconditional love a mother has for a child." After "my world collapsed," Bono began to write about death, the reigning motif of U2's first album, *Boy* (1980).[6]

But in 1974, "the death of my mother really affected my confidence. I would go back to my house after school, but it wasn't a home. She was gone. . . . I felt abandoned, afraid. I guess fear converts to anger pretty quickly. It's still with me," he confessed in 2005. His lack of confidence, however, also fed Bono's need to be around others, the center of attention. He gave money to friends who couldn't afford groceries. He engaged in petty theft. And he fought with his strict father, even once throwing a knife at him. "I think both of us wept, and both of us admitted that we were just angry at each other because we didn't know how to grieve."[7]

The members of U2 were also exposed early on to poverty. To be sure, their own families were relatively comfortable, the Hewsons living in a neighborhood of semidetached homes with gardens, lawns, and driveways.[8] "I grew up on Cedarwood Road," Bono recalled. "[A] nice street with nice families. People who shaped my world view. People I still admire and love."[9] The Evanses were solidly middle class, the father an engineer. Adam's father was a pilot. As Bono recalled, however, he was never certain whether he was "working class or middle class."[10] U2 were exposed to the nearby Ballymun Flats, built in 1967 to move thousands from city slums into "seven towers" of which U2 would later sing in "Running to Stand Still" about heroin addiction, a widespread and devastating affliction in Dublin. In the 1970s, the towers were a reminder that Ireland remained the poorest nation in Western Europe, "small and insulated" to boot.[11] Paul was also angry at the environmental damage done by Dublin buildings, the tearing of trees "to build an awful development."[12]

Out of poverty came violence. Dubliners were safely 60-odd miles from the terror in Northern Ireland, which, according to biographer John Waters, placed U2 in "that generation of young Irish people which had its own experience of being isolated behind the lies of a war in which it was not involved."[13] Bono admitted in 1981 being unaware of The Troubles.[14] When asked if the war affected him much, The Edge explained, "I would personally feel, not that much directly, there's much more of an undertone to the way of life in Dublin. We've said in interviews that the bombs don't go off in Dublin, but some of them are certainly made here. There is that sort of backdrop to your life."[15] According to childhood friend Neil McCormick, 1970s Irish teenagers were less ideological than their parents. "Older generations might have had strong political feelings . . . but politically and economically, the Republic of Ireland had its own issues to deal with, and there was more of a sense of paying lip service to the notion of a united Ireland. . . . There was no bombing in the south, no sectarian murder, and no soldiers on the street to contend with."[16]

Except that there was a bombing in the south. On May 17, 1974, coordinated car bombs went off in Dublin and Monaghan, both in the Republic of Ireland. They killed 33 people, ranging in age from five months to 80 years, and an unborn child. Almost 300 more bystanders were injured, many blasted into shop windows. The Ulster Volunteer Force, loyalist paramilitaries from Northern Ireland, claimed responsibility in 1993. Three of the four bombs went off in Dublin during rush hour. The second one exploded on Talbot Street and killed 14, including a woman nine months pregnant. Thirteen of the 14 dead were women. Bono typically would have been on Talbot Street around that time, but, perhaps because of an ongoing bus strike, "I rode my bike to school that day and dodged one of the bloodiest moments in a history that divided an island," he wrote in the liner notes of *Songs of Innocence.* "My old friend Andy Rowen (Guck Pants Delaney we used to call him) was locked in his father's van as his dad ran to help save the victims Scattered [*sic*] like refuse across the street. . . . The scene never left him, he turned to one of the worlds [*sic*] great painkillers to deal with it"—heroin.

Far from actual war, Dublin boys still lived in a harsh world. "You have to remember where we came from or where I came from at least," Bono said in 2000. "We came from nowhere. We came from this place that was just grey concrete, lower middle class, a ghetto of non-culture. The thing I remember the most about growing up is violence."[17] "It was a warzone in my teens," Bono sings on "Cedarwood Road," and, again in his liner notes for *Songs of Innocence*, Bono recalled that "Ireland in the 70s was a tough place. . . . There was a lot of violence near by in my teenage years . . . skinheads and boot boys, blades and knuckledusters. Teenage parties where boys would turn up with hammers and saws." "Street fights were just the way," Bono also recollected. "I remember picking up a dustbin [garbage can] in a street fight, and I remember thinking to myself, 'This is ridiculous. I'm not going to hit someone with this.' And right then, this guy came up with an iron bar and brought that iron bar down so hard on me. And I just used the lid to protect myself. I would have been dead, stone dead, if I hadn't had that thing."[18] Paul had his own anger to unleash. When a neighborhood ruffian bit his friend's ear, "I took that kid's head and banged it off the iron railing."[19] With skinheads roaming Dublin, he recalled, "I would worry sick about having to go out on the street."[20] Even as U2, young thugs stalked them and called them "Protestant bastards," a class-based insult more than anything else.[21]

Faced with two warring factions, "peace seemed possible through only a third way: a rejection of things as they stood," reflected McCormick. "So in a sense, the presence of the Northern Ireland Troubles helped shape a political character that rejected the status quo, a character that is apparent in U2."[22]

Much of the band's rebellion found positive outlets in a secondary school called Mount Temple, special for being beyond the Church's reach. The "One True Church," as Catholicism was still called in the 1970s, educated 95 percent of the Irish.[23] It dominated society and government and outlawed divorce, homosexuality, abortion, contraception, and pornography. "My friends and I understood," wrote McCormick of Ireland, "that it was not a fundamentally modern country."[24] Bono initially spent an unhappy year at St. Patrick's secondary school, unable to adhere to its formalities. He misbehaved, was caught throwing feces at his Spanish teacher, and was told he could not return the following year.[25]

U2 luckily escaped the fate of most Irish teens because of the high school in which Paul ended up. More than anything, Mount Temple gave the future bandmates the freedom and openness to find their place in the world.[26] As luck would have it, this alternative secondary school opened its doors in 1972 as the first comprehensive, nondenominational, coeducational school in Dublin just as Paul needed to leave St. Patrick's. Students, most of them Protestant, read Canadian Leonard Cohen's erotic poetry in class and sat through a sex education lecture "so explicit that it caused one nervous girl to faint."[27] Music teacher Albert Bradshaw introduced many to choir and told Dave Evans and his brother Dick about young Larry Mullen's famous bulletin board note about wanting to form a band.[28] Donald Moxham, their history teacher, taught the musicians about the world and gave them a room in which to practice. Dress codes were loose, and Adam took full advantage of them to wear a kilt.[29] English teacher and guidance counselor Jack Heaslip helped Paul deal with his grief and "gave Bono a lot of time and space to work things out for himself," according to McCormick. Heaslip went on to become an Anglican priest who officiated at Bono's wedding, baptized his children, and buried his father.[30]

The middle-class Mount Temple kids had other advantages. Ireland was poor, to be sure, but increasingly connected to the world. Its growing economy attracted well-off immigrants from the United Kingdom. Pirate radio and television antennae connected the Irish to the British Broadcasting Channel and thus to global news.[31] The Irish, finally, had the great fortune of speaking English.

McCormick recalled how Paul both suffered and benefited from "a fear of repose." His "sense of loss and injustice" over his mother's death made of him "a bit of a star in the corridors of Mount Temple. . . . He was the kind of boy people wanted to know."[32] Paul flirted with being an actor. Mostly, he believed in inclusion and developed a hatred of bigotry. When Paul found music and assumed the name Bono given to him by friend Gavin Friday, he looked up to Bruce Springsteen, "the Buddha of my youth," for his independence, integrity, and meaningful songs in an otherwise egotistical music business.[33]

Much of that selfishness seemed paradoxically embodied by punk music, an early but ambivalent influence on the budding musicians. When the Ramones and the Clash exploded onto the music scene in 1976 and 1977, the four Mount Temple kids who could barely play their instruments fed off punk's energy and individualism. The Clash, recalled Bono in 2012, "gave U2 the idea that social activism could make for a very musical riot."[34] In 2014, U2 dedicated songs to Joey Ramone and to the Clash's Joe Strummer. "You could hear an echo of your pain in his voice," Bono recalled of the first. "That's why you believed in him, surfing to the future on a sea of noise." U2 snuck into a Ramones show in Dublin, and "it became one of the great nights of our life. . . . After the Ramones, I could try and be myself as a singer. I just needed to find out who that was . . . emancipation." Strummer, meanwhile, was explicitly political, "some soldier," Bono called him. "His guitar a weapon, his mouth almighty. [W]e weren't sure exactly what they were fighting for/ against but this was a public announcement with guitars on behalf of the soul and we signed up."[35]

But punk's cynicism and nihilism escaped them. "It was sad for us in U2 to discover when we were 18 that the Sex Pistols were a 'good idea' that someone had thought up," said Bono, referring to the fact that the band's image as rebels was partly a marketing ploy by their manager. "Because when we were 16 we had believed in it, we believed in rock & roll." "The Sex Pistols were a con, a box of tricks sold by Malcolm McLaren. Kids were sold the imagery of violence, which turned into the reality of violence. . . . People like Bruce Springsteen carry hope. Like the

Who—'Won't Get Fooled Again.' I mean, there is a song of endurance, and that's the attitude of the great bands." For such attitudes, *Rolling Stone* described U2 as "postalienationist," celebrating "communion over segregation, compassion over blame, hope over despair."[36]

A year and a half after forming a band and calling themselves Feedback and then The Hype, the boys settled on the name U2, partly because it eluded any obvious stylistic category and because it expressed the band's desire to reach out to audiences during its live shows. It was Bono's engagement with those audiences, particularly his insistence on making eye contact—a rare trait in singers at that time—that convinced Paul McGuinness to manage U2.[37]

U2, however, had yet to come fully to terms with its religiosity. Bono shared his parents' disdain for organized religion, which he felt kept Protestants and Catholics petty and hateful. "In their relationship," he said of Bob and Iris, "they were proof that the bitterness between those two communities is ridiculous."[38] "I grew up with the sense that if my faith meant anything, it must be tackling inequality."[39] It was at Mount Temple that Paul first saw in Christianity an uplifting side. Nearly half the school was undergoing a religious experience, he recalled.[40] Around 15, Paul joined its Christian Union, an evangelical student group. Prayer meetings took place in the mornings, and at lunch 100 students or more would gather for praise. Bono would show up at beach barbecues to pray and sing.[41] The school was never dogmatic, instead showing its teens a progressive side to faith. Mount Temple graduates rarely grew to hate Catholicism; they embraced its humanistic teachings and its calls to action. The Hype played their first benefit gig in 1978 for the Contraception Action Campaign.

The evangelical wave washing over Mount Temple extended to Ireland as a whole in 1976. One of its results was the formation of Shalom, a Charismatic Christian worship group whose name means "peace" in Hebrew. Of the U2 crew who joined after high school were The Edge, Larry, Bono's girlfriend Alison "Ali" Stewart, and Bono himself, who portrayed Shalom as "Catholics and Protestants in Ireland worshipping God together in a kind of hippy rave format, minus the beats per minute."[42] Biographer Eamon Dunphy described twice-weekly prayer meetings as filled with gospel songs and gentle, values-focused Bible readings:

There was no fire-and-brimstone preaching, no symbolic paraphernalia at these Meetings. . . . There was a spirit of humility, a sense of God in the form of goodness being present. . . . In a world where family life was breaking down, which was preoccupied by the make of car you drove, the type of Spanish holiday you went on, a world of hi-fi, portable color TV, where sexual fidelity was a joke, Christianity was a balm for the more sensitive spirit. [43]

"I nearly became a full time instead of part-time activist at that point," Bono later admitted. [44] He and The Edge were even baptized in the sea. With Larry, they would be up at 5:00 a.m. to study the Bible. [45] Part of U2's motivation for joining Shalom was that "we were angry. We were agitated by the inequalities in the world and the lack of a spiritual life." [46] Shalom influenced the title of U2's second album, *October* (1981), which to Bono signified that the early 1980s were a dark era, "after the fall, after the harvest." The spread of middle-class comforts in the 1960s had given way to "materialism without any idealism." Technology was used almost exclusively for military might rather than helping the jobless and the hungry. [47]

However, U2 broke with even this loosely organized religious group. While the band was on tour between *Boy* and *October*, some members of Shalom directed U2 to give up their godless, rock-and-roll ways. The three U2 members of Shalom, agreeing that band life might conflict with religion, almost followed orders.

"Then," recalled Bono, "we came to a realization: 'hold on a second. Where are these gifts coming from? This is how we worship God, even though we don't write religious songs, because we didn't feel God needs the advertising.'" [48] Manager McGuinness, a lapsed Catholic, reminded them of the commitments they had made to their musical community and helped them come to the conclusion that God and music could coexist. Adam, the nonbeliever of the group, was greatly relieved when the three others chose the band rather than Shalom. It was a seminal moment in U2's definition of community as intimate while ambitiously expansive.

Without Shalom, the members of U2 had, besides each other, another group with which to identify. Lypton Village, as they called it, was a tight-knit nonviolent "gang" that included U2 and the Virgin Prunes, a more avant-garde, theatrical band who were childhood friends of Bono's. Lypton Village reacted to what Bono saw as a "bland," fundamentalist, superficial society of 1970s Ireland by creating an alternative community

engaging in absurd humor. More seriously, Gavin Friday of the Virgin
Prunes rejected the intense nationalism in Ireland that he blamed for
much of the violence. "I don't see anywhere as being separate. Ireland is
there and the people there are as important as the people in Hong Kong or
Belgium. All this trip of 'I'm Irish' or 'I'm English,' it's not important. . . . I don't like nationalities."[49] By pursuing the spirit of community
at home while letting go of imagined communities imposed by others,
U2's global identity was in the works.[50]

As their musical careers flourished, the four young men abjured most
manners of vice. "We were confused by the sexual revolution," Adam
admitted. "Promiscuity didn't appeal to us. And neither did the drug
culture—longhaired people smoking pot and talking about the cosmos."[51]
"The whole drug culture is a criminal thing," added The Edge. "The same
guys who deal the marijuana are the guys who deal heroin, who break
people's legs, who get 13 year olds hooked. I felt no attraction to that side
of it." To young Bono, the lot of most Irish youths was not for U2:
"drinking Thursday night, drinking Friday . . . Saturday night, drinking
Sunday. . . . We would see this. And we just said, 'We will not become a
part of this.'"[52] Pubs "looked like a trapdoor to somewhere very predict-
able, so we wouldn't drink. We used to watch Monty Python. We invent-
ed our own language, gave each other names, and we'd dress differently."

U2 also refused to sleep with female fans. "Sexual favors traded for
proximity with the band, it sounds like a turnoff to me," said Bono.
"When there is no equality in the relationship it's less interesting. Taking
advantage of a fan, sexual bullying is to be avoided."[53] Larry was especially vigilant about the "no groupies" rule backstage.

"I questioned even things like smoking," said Bono. "I got bored very
quickly with those terms of rebellion because, unlike my neighbors, I
wasn't being told all the time not to do this." The band, whom journalist
Bill Graham described as "early risers and early sleepers," never trashed a
hotel room.[54] To be sure, they eventually enjoyed a few drinks, perhaps a
few joints. But only Adam was ever arrested for drug possession (of
marijuana), and only he ever missed a concert (because of a wicked
hangover).

Rebellion, to U2, was not about escapism. It was about values and
action. "I think that, ultimately, the group is totally rebellious because of
our stance against what people accept as rebellion," said Bono. "I'm not
interested in politics like people fighting back with sticks and stones, but

in the politics of love." Speaking to *Rolling Stone* while touring Margaret Thatcher's Britain in 1981, Bono knew that in his audience of 17- to 25-year-olds, "there is massive unemployment, and there is real disillusionment. U2's music is about getting up and doing something about it."[55]

U2 also spent its early years defining itself in relation to Ireland, the United Kingdom, and the United States. Despite their claim to know little about Ireland, U2 had already rebelled against traditional Irish society. The music business also made it difficult for a rock act to stay in Ireland. Government had a monopoly on television and radio, which thus ignored rock and roll. There was no popular music press except for the embryonic *Hot Press* magazine, which early on promoted the band.[56] If they did become big, rock acts found few concert venues beyond church halls, community centers, and parking lots. "International bands rarely visited," recalled McCormick. "There were some theaters, some big pub venues, and a boxing ring." McCormick warns not to "overstate our isolation. We could find records imported. . . . We had some rebel rock radio. . . . But there was nonetheless a scarcity to it that made it more precious and more baffling."[57]

London was the logical step up for a successful Irish act, but the scene there, to U2 and McGuinness, seemed parochial, suffocating, and prejudiced against the Irish. London tended to catapult bands to fame before they were ready and then chew them up. So, although they toured considerably in England, Bono and his mates remained headquartered in Ireland until they were ready for the U.S. market, where local radio promoted bands, which had to tour ceaselessly and earn their way to the top. U2 was ready for the challenge.

U2 truly gained a loyal transatlantic audience by playing live. It was in its shows that U2's sense of community shone. Fans of punk or New Wave music were used to stone-faced musicians who turned their backs to them or rabid ones who cursed and spit at them. Not U2. Bono's stage presence was all about communication. He articulated lyrics, looked the audience in the eyes, and made everyone in the room, even those at the back, feel they were in an intimate venue. U2 even allowed radio listeners to choose its singles.[58] American audiences loved U2. In Boston, one of their first U.S. gigs, the audience demanded three encores.[59] From March to May 1981, they played 61 shows in North America. At a small club in deeply religious Oklahoma City, one fan was "transfixed" by U2:

The energy with which they played, the vulnerability with which Bono interacted with the audience and the band's almost-painful sincerity instead of the usual rock poses of irony and superiority transformed that dingy club into something that . . . I would have recognized: a place of worship. . . . We in the audience were also transformed. We sensed our better natures, our connection to one another and to the world, and while they were playing, I honestly believed that—in the right hands—rock 'n' roll could change the world, because for an hour and a half, it had certainly changed us. [60]

* * *

As 1983 began, U2 could have been pessimistic because *October* had received mixed reviews and sold less than *Boy*. Yet the band imagined a bright future for themselves. They had been embraced by fans around the world while being admired as an Irish band. They had maintained their integrity in the music business. And their religious faith moved them toward compassion and action without limiting their possibilities. "I think the important thing to retain through life is optimism," said Adam in 1982. "It doesn't have to be something that you necessarily get from Christianity. You just have to feel that way about life." "We refute the belief that man is just a higher stage of animal, that he has no spirit," added Bono. "I think that when people start believing that, the real respect for humanity is gone. You are just a cog in a wheel, another collection of molecules. That's half the reason for a lot of the pessimism in the world."[61] U2 refused to be cogs in anyone's wheel.

2

THE RAISING OF A GLOBAL CONSCIOUSNESS, 1983–1989

Who can argue about human rights? It's fundamental.—The Edge[1]

From 1983's *War* album to 1989's *Rattle and Hum*, U2 rapidly ascended and arrived at the pinnacle of rock superstardom. The 1980s was also the decade in which U2 moved beyond Irish venues and Irish issues and became global activists. They represented—and to a large degree led—a revival of social consciousness in popular music, choosing to place themselves at the center of almost every event dedicated to raising consciousness, raising money, and raising hell against the decade's descent into materialism, militarism, and cynicism. Festival after festival, tour after tour, they publicized every struggle under the sun—against hunger, war, and racism and in defense of prisoners of conscience. Throughout it all, U2 sought to make respect for human rights a tenet of international politics. As The Edge's epigraph suggested, however, embracing something as fundamental as human rights seemed inarguable and thus relatively "safe" for budding activists. The 1980s proved a vital step into the complex, frustrating world of global activism.

* * *

In 1989, Bono looked back and concluded that "the '80s have been a blight, culturally and socio-politically. . . . And I'm personally embarrassed that we're 'the band of the '80s.'"[2]

That moniker referred not only to U2's musical influence—the band had a defined "sound" copied by many—but also to its efforts to bring a social conscience back to popular music. In the 1960s and early 1970s, the civil rights and anti–Vietnam War movements galvanized musicians into speaking out, but the mid-1970s brought what writer Carter Alan called "a flight from reality, with popular music refocusing on escapist lyrics and sentiments." The punk explosion of 1976–1977 was quickly followed by "a brief period of flowery, dance-oriented new wave." The U2-led return of activist music included the Gang of Four, the English Beat, the Clash, and the Dead Kennedys.[3] All addressed in some way the political, spiritual, and emotional longing of "a generation without name, ripped and torn," as U2 sang in "Like a Song" from *War*. "It's fair to say that U2 were part of creating . . . this kind of positive protest movement in the Eighties" to change "the wickedness of the world."[4]

Bono often spoke of his technique to have music lead to change not by chanting shopworn political slogans but rather by articulating emotions emerging from political conflict. "Half of me says I know I can't change the world and there's another half of me that, every time I write a song I want it to change the world," he said in 1982. "I don't know if that's naivety or stupidity in me but I do know that music has changed me and I know that in Vietnam music helped change a generation's attitudes. . . . What's important is the individual, that's where you start."[5] Individuals in the midst of difficult social or political circumstances were often U2's topics in songs such as "New Year's Day" or "Red Hill Mining Disaster." They allowed the band to reach audiences through emotions and poetry rather than through the impersonal, preachy lyrics of a Billy Bragg or a Phil Ochs.

In 1983, with *War* released in February and a North American tour launched in April, the first social issues that U2 tackled concerned, logically enough, Ireland and Irishness in America. "When we first started touring Britain and Europe, we started seeing how Irish we were. Suddenly, Ireland became big in our songs. When we first toured America, we sensed our Europeaness," recalled The Edge years later.[6] *War* was a far more openly political record than *Boy* or *October* had been. Its songs spoke of the dangers brought forth by mostly new conservative governments—the Falklands/Malvinas war between Margaret Thatcher's United Kingdom and Argentina; the possible nuclear apocalypse, brought closer by Thatcher's decision to install U.S. Pershing cruise missiles in Britain;

the indifference to war of 1980s youth mesmerized by television; the anticommunist Solidarity movement in Poland; and, still, war in Northern Ireland.[7] "War seemed to be the motif for 1982," reflected Bono. "Everywhere you looked, from the Falklands to the Middle East to South Africa, there was war."[8] Redemption, indicated "Sunday, Bloody Sunday," came in following Jesus' pacifist example.

Yet the album opened up U2 to misinterpretation. The band's 1982 experience of almost marching in a New York City parade alongside Irish Republican Army (IRA) associates prompted them not only to write "Sunday, Bloody Sunday," which recalled British armed forces massacres against unarmed civilians in 1972 and 1921, but also to refuse to take sides in the Catholic–Protestant conflict.[9] Before every performance, it seemed, Bono had to state that the song "is not a rebel song." Soon the band were "deliberately trying to dry up funds for the IRA in America" because of its terrorist tactics.[10] In 2010, Bono celebrated British Prime Minister David Cameron's apology for Bloody Sunday.[11]

Bono was burned again by Irish politics when he agreed to serve on a youth unemployment committee for the Irish government. In his telling, fellow committee members resisted his idea to consult with the actual unemployed.[12]

So when this Irish band toured the United States, spelling out its stance on Irish politics was akin to walking a tightrope. "America had quite a distorted idea, a romantic idea, of what the IRA were on about," said Bono. "And they tried to imbue us with this kind of street-fighting Irish credibility." Bono started throwing back into the audience Irish flags that landed on his stage, expressing outrage that, as he said, "nationalism has betrayed the nation."[13] White flags soon replaced those of nation-states. "The whole idea of the white flag on stage was to get away from Green White and Orange, to get away from the Stars and Stripes, to get away from the Union Jack. I am an Irishman and we are an Irish group—stop! But I'm frightened of borders, frightened of restrictions on those levels."[14]

When Gerry Adams, the leader of Sinn Fein, the political arm of the IRA, learned of U2's neutrality, he tore the U2 poster from his Dublin office and called Bono "a little shit." U2 also received kidnapping threats, and supporters of the Provos, or the Provisional IRA, once surrounded their car.[15] In 1987, during the recording of the *Joshua Tree* tour for the

"Rattle and Hum" documentary, an IRA bomb killed 18 people in Enniskillen, leading Bono to shout from the stage, "Fuck the revolution!"

Although U2's take on Irish politics became clear enough by the mid-1980s, the band seemed to have grown cautious of aligning themselves with any political faction or campaign. It was perhaps for this reason that they clung to the more cautious catchall of human rights.

U2's openness and intimacy, interpreted as letting go of Europeanness just as they were supposedly discovering it, helped win over audiences who didn't much care about Irish issues anyway. "I remember playing our first tour of the United States," recalled Bono. "There might be like sixty, seventy, one hundred people in the club. The floor would be empty. I would leave the stage, sit at their tables, drink their drinks and kiss their girlfriends. Fun stuff. I loved that. I loved becoming the audience."[16] "Here was a European band," biographer Eamon Dunphy writes, "that *wasn't* condescending, as desperate to be loved and accepted as the audience, in the first year of Ronald Reagan, was to see and feel something real, not plastic, something human and uncontrived. Bono and U2 were it."[17] Bono often stopped a show cold because he observed some fighting in the back rows. "We do not have violence at U2 gigs," he once instructed. "Not ever. Enough!" Immediately, the tussle stopped.[18]

Even with 1987's *The Joshua Tree*, U2's attacks on U.S. militarism in Central America and elsewhere were well received by audiences. Niall Stokes and Bill Graham saw the album as free "of the condescension and detachment which so often characterizes the UK rock perspective on the United States and its people. The Irish don't view America like the Brits." U2 released *Joshua Tree* amid the Iran-Contra scandal, which revealed how the Reagan administration sold arms to terrorists and diverted the profits to counterrevolutionaries, both policies nakedly contrary to Reagan's public declarations and to legislation passed by Congress. "'The Joshua Tree,'" continued Stokes and Graham, "is about articulating the sense of outrage which America's unique combination of arrogance and apathy inspires from an Irish perspective. . . . In a world where power is abused on a colossal scale and people are trampled into the dust without compunction by political and economic masters who have lost all sense of human dignity, U2 have sought and found the ultimate symbol of triumph over adversity. 'The Joshua Tree' is about the belief that you cannot kill the human spirit."[19]

U2 also spent the 1980s on an assault on U.S. religious hypocrisy. That decade's television preachers were a particularly loathsome lot, exploiting viewers' devoutness and ignorance to collect donations in the name of God. *October*, released in late 1981, had its dark sides, but its approach to religion had been largely celebratory because U2 were unaware of born-again Christianity's capture by righteousness and materialist selfishness outside of Ireland.

They found out in an early tour of the United States when critics equated them with right-wing fundamentalists. And so Bono inserted a monologue about television preachers in "Bullet the Blue Sky" and denounced "televangelists" in interview after interview. Once again, he transposed his Irish background onto his American experiences. "I'm frightened by religion, I've seen what it's done to this country," Bono told an Irish reporter. "I go to America and I turn on my television set and I start sweating profusely because those guys have turned faith into an industry. It's appalling."[20] "What's always bothered me about the fundamentalists is that they seem preoccupied with the most obvious of sins [such as] sexual immorality and drug addiction. . . . The same people were never questioning the deeper, slyer problems of the human spirit like self-righteousness, judgmentalism, institutional greed, corporate greed."[21] "The Jesus Christ I believe in was the man who turned over the tables in the temple and threw the moneychangers out."[22]

The Edge later railed against Jerry Falwell, leader of the Moral Majority, a conservative Christian lobbying group that led the charge in forcing fundamentalist precepts into U.S. politics. To the guitarist, Falwell preached the ludicrous notion that "God dresses in a three-piece polyester suit, is white, speaks in a Southern accent, is from an Anglo-Saxon background and has a wife and children. And then you say, how that relates to a Chinese peasant and you realize it doesn't relate at all."

A global consciousness was seeping into U2's worldview. As The Edge explained, "The principles must be universal to be understood and appreciated and if that's not the case, it's not worth a shit."[23]

U2's encounter with the United States also confronted it with the inevitable issue of race. Bono's frustrations with Reagan foreign policy led him to seek a brighter side to U.S. politics, and he found it in the civil rights activism of Martin Luther King Jr. The band visited the Chicago Peace Museum, and the result was "Pride (In the Name of Love)," their first hit and one of their most poignant songs.[24] *The Unforgettable Fire*

(1984), of which "Pride" was the first single, was less aggressive than *War* but still inspired by social issues, such as heroin addiction in Ireland and atomic devastation. Yet it was the memory and message of King that dominated the album. "Because of the situation in our country," The Edge explained, "non-violent struggle was such an inspiring concept."[25] U2 donated several items to a Peace Museum exhibit in 1983 called "Give Peace a Chance." One of the donations was a Bono poem, "Dreams in a Box," which partly went as follows:

> We know that peace is a living thing
>
> . . . .
>
> That it does not bow down to Marx or Lenin, Reagan or Thatcher
> That it is not infected by hypodermic needles
> And yet it must infect us with a cure, contagious.
> Peace will not prosper while the poor are controlled in ghettos
> Cornered by color or greed,
> From Watts to Harlem, Belfast to Beirut
> We must find new solutions to new problems.[26]

Hot Press writers Niall Stokes and Dermot Stokes took from U2's association with King that "the message of U2's music—that we must wrestle with the demons of violence and hatred and aggression and that we must win, peacefully . . . can hardly be lost on the people of Dublin."[27]

U2 also began to see in the 1980s that their growing influence could not only raise political awareness but also move political needles. In 1982, Bono ran into Garret Fitzgerald, leader of the Fine Gael party who was running for taioseach, or Irish prime minister. Fitzgerald soon after visited U2 at their recording studio, and photographers were there to capture a moment splashed onto every front page in Ireland. Fitzgerald won the election the following week. He called Bono's kind words about his party "politically helpful."[28]

The period from 1984 to 1986 was particularly dynamic for U2's activism. The band embraced a host of causes and helped raise for them not only awareness but also money. The first such endeavor was Band Aid in late 1984. Fellow Irishman Bob Geldof of the Boomtown Rats gathered British pop stars to record a musically uplifting "Do They Know It's Christmas?" Its cause was the famine in Ethiopia, which television images had recently brought into the living rooms of the West. The single rocketed to number one and raised £8 million.

Bono felt awkward in the studio, surrounded by bigger stars, such as Boy George, Simon LeBon, George Michael, and Phil Collins. He felt that U2 "were part of the changing of the climate" toward a more socially conscious music world, yet "it was incredibly uncool to make this record." Sting and The Police, for instance, "were doing the de-do-do-do/de-da-da-das! So this was a break, this was not cool—for a band to take this position. But every so often rock and roll is allowed to be earnest."[29]

Some critics had problems not with the earnestness but rather with the ignorant and paternalistic lyrics of "Do They Know It's Christmas?," beginning with the title. Decades later, writer Harry Browne noted how, in the song, "Africa itself is essentialised as a nightmarish place of undifferentiated poverty ('where nothing ever grows, no rain or rivers flow'); and Westerners are cast as their saviors, the people who will give them both physical sustenance and spiritual uplift." In his opinion, these visions bore "a striking resemblance to the dominant themes of Bono's African work in the decades that followed."[30]

Read as irony, Bono's single line in the song, *Well tonight, thank God it's them, instead of you,* foreshadowed his own revulsion at the selfishness of the West when facing African suffering. But the irony wasn't clear at first. Before the recording, he was ready to sing any lyric except that one. Yet Geldof insisted that he sing "this fucking line here" and berated Bono, "This is not about what you want, OK? This is about what these people need." Bono observed how the line "reveals how selfish a mindset we all have underneath."

And, as always, U2 thought about how they reflected their times. Adam added that perhaps the popularity of the single "was a reaction to the years of Thatcherism, when you knew that a Conservative government wasn't likely to take much interest in the plight of Africans."[31]

Live Aid soon followed Band Aid. On July 13, 1985, over 2 billion people watched on television as rock stars and movie stars in stadium concerts in London and Philadelphia raised over $200 million for Ethiopian famine relief. U2 were hardly chart toppers at the time. That all changed when Bono, in the middle of singing the rather obscure "Bad" about heroin addiction, spontaneously burned through several minutes of precious stage time to leap off the stage and dance with a young female fan (see figure 2.1). His intent was merely to bring to the enormous Wembley Stadium the intimacy of U2's live shows. "By holding onto this person, I felt like I was holding onto the whole audience."[32] But time had run out to play their only hit, "Pride." The rest of the band was "very, very upset—they nearly fired me," recalled Bono.[33]

Yet U2 found that audiences craved such moments of intimacy between those on the stage and those in the seats, an expression of the humanity at the heart of the fund-raiser itself. They were universally praised as giving one of the two best performances of the day (the other was from Queen), all their albums raced back into the charts, and their record sales tripled in the months that followed.[34] The Irish also donated more money per capita to Live Aid than any other nation, almost a pound per person.[35]

The band released the statement that the Live Aid concerts were "a demonstration to the politicians and policy-makers that men, women and children will not walk by other men, women and children as they lie bellies swollen, starving to death for the sake of a cup of grain and water. . . . For the price of Star Wars [the Reagan administration's outer-space antimissile system], the MX missile offensive-defense budgets, the deserts of Africa could be turned into fertile lands. The technology is with

Figure 2.1.   U2 at Live Aid, Wembley Stadium, London, July 13, 1985. Bono is signaling for the security staff to pull a fan out of the audience. *Nils Jorgensen/ Richard Young/REX*

us. The technocrats are not. Are we part of a civilization that protects itself by investing in life . . . or investing in death?"[36]

Bono was at this early stage showing the mixture of anger and optimism that would mark his later lobbying of "technocrats." He was also moved by the mid-nineteenth-century famine in Ireland that halved its population.[37] Besides raising funds, Band Aid, Live Aid, and other African relief movements changed attitudes of Western governments wary of sending aid to communist governments in the Horn of Africa. As a result, notes one scholar, "20 fixed-wing aircraft and 30 helicopters from the UK, USA, USSR, FRG [West Germany], and GDR [East Germany], Italy and Libya were involved in airlifting supplies."[38]

Live Aid inspired Bono himself to do more than sing and send out press releases. "I just can't get these people I'm seeing on television out of my head," he told Ali, who was now his wife. "We have to try and do something." Invited by charity organizations such as World Vision and Concern, the Hewsons airlifted themselves to Ethiopia, thus solidifying an emotional commitment to Africa that would translate into action again more than a decade later. They spent five weeks around September 1985 in country, mostly in a feeding center and orphanage in Ajibar. "We lived in a little tent," recalled Bono. "The camp was surrounded by barbed wire. Woke up in the mornings as the mist lifted, and watched thousands of Africans, who had walked all night with the little belongings they had, coming toward us to beg for food and their life. . . . For a couple of kids from the suburbs, it was a very overwhelming experience." As for work, Bono and Ali shoveled dirt, but they also wrote songs and playlets meant to encourage healthy habits—eating vegetables, washing hands, and so on. On this trip, Bono was uncharacteristically media shy and didn't talk publicly about it for two years until photographs he took there went on display.[39] "A lot of people would give their right arms to go to Ethiopia and help out. I could afford to," he remarked. He also wanted to avoid offending nonfamous aid workers.[40]

His most trying experience in Ethiopia was when a father with a starving child begged Bono to adopt him. "Please, take my boy, because if he stays with me, he will surely die. If he goes with you, he will live," the father told Bono, who reflected, "Having to say no, and having to turn away, is a very . . . very, very, very, very hard thing to do."[41] On his return, Bono was humbled, saying, "I got more than I gave to Ethiopia."

He was also angry about

spending time in Africa and seeing people in the pits of poverty. I still saw a very strong spirit in the people, a richness of spirit I didn't see when I came home. I had no culture shock going, but I had culture shock coming back. I saw the spoiled child of the Western world. I started thinking, "They may have a physical desert, but we've got other kinds of deserts." And that's what attracted me to the desert as a symbol of some sort.[42]

The feeling that the West was "spiritually impoverished" inspired the song "Where the Streets Have No Name."[43]

Perhaps the most crucial lessons about Ethiopia for Bono were the causes of poverty: civil war, natural disasters, and the corruption of wealthy governments whose hold on poor ones stemmed from trade agreements and debt.[44] Bono insisted on the good that the organizations he worked with were doing and saw firsthand the improvement that can come from donations. He felt uncomfortable taking photos of the sick, so he focused on those who regained health because of their treatment. He thereafter often made a point of praising the beauty and nobility of Africans, "to describe Africa in terms other than tragedy."[45] Adam Clayton also had a positive experience with Africa due to childhood years in Kenya.[46]

As late as 2013, Bono assessed that his 1985 Ethiopia trip "turned my life upside down."[47]

Before the trip, U2 had already participated in protest marches against the racist regime in 1980s South Africa.[48] The day after he returned to Dublin from Ethiopia, Bono got a call from Artists United Against Apartheid and flew to New York. He helped record the single "Sun City" and wrote and recorded, with Keith Richards and Ron Wood of the Rolling Stones, "Silver and Gold" to encourage artists, academics, and athletes to boycott the country and to raise an eventual $1 million for the Africa Fund for antiapartheid causes. U2 themselves "many times" turned down white South African invitations to play in the country.[49] South Africa's Archbishop Desmond Tutu admitted he was "very, very impressed with [U2's] social consciousness. They were very strongly aware of the anti-apartheid struggles, which they supported and this is something that thrilled us."[50]

When South Africa dismantled apartheid in the 1990s, the first band that the majority-black African National Congress invited to play in the country was U2.[51]

The summer of 1986 was the busiest of the decade for U2's activism. It began on May 17, when the band headlined Self Aid, Ireland's largest-ever concert. Its strategy was unique: To address the 15 to 20 percent unemployment rate in Ireland, which tens of thousands left each year out of desperation, concert organizers encouraged viewers to phone in job offers. In front of 30,000 fans and an additional 1 million on television, the band turned in a searing performance of Bob Dylan's "Maggie's Farm" to express their anger at Irish emigration to the United Kingdom, what The Edge called "the most difficult underground problem in this society."[52] The show raised $1 million and created over 1,200 jobs.[53]

However, the Irish media this time turned on the band, accusing them of helping the government shirk its responsibility for job creation by foisting it on the private sector. Journalists parodied the concert's slogan, "Make It Work," by substituting "Self Aid Makes It Worse."[54] Defenders responded that U2 "weren't bull believers in every aspect of the event.[55] U2's good intentions had run up against social democracy's struggle against the selfishness of modern capitalism—the despair in seeing government using philanthropy to abandon its role as provider for the needy. The accusation would grow louder in the twenty-first century.

Nevertheless, U2's activism soon took on a new commitment—to Amnesty International. In 1986, the organization defending prisoners of conscience wished to celebrate its quarter century with a tour. As with South Africa, the band was aware of the situation beforehand, Bono having heard of Amnesty through the 1979 movie *The Secret Policeman's Ball*. "It sowed a seed," he recalled. "Any criticism of this tour being ineffective in raising awareness is unfair," Bono notes. "I'm the perfect argument against that."[56] U2 had also donated proceeds from a 1984 show to Amnesty.

Amnesty's Irish American executive director of the U.S. branch and a former monk, Jack Healey, had seen U2 live, and it convinced him that "this band could carry the message of human rights."[57] Healey approached Paul McGuinness with an invitation to join a tour to boost the 150,000-strong Amnesty membership in the United States. "You guys can help us break out into the open," said Healey. The manager immediately committed the band.[58] "I knew the human rights movement really changed that day," Healey later said.[59] U2 made phone calls, and soon several other bands joined the tour (see figure 2.2). Many musicians recorded video messages, AT&T provided an 800 number for donations, and the Hyatt Corporation rented hotel rooms for free.[60]

Eventually, the six shows in San Francisco, Los Angeles, Denver, Atlanta, Chicago, and New Jersey drew $3 million to $5 million in donations, and the last show, on June 15, 1986, was broadcast on national television and radio. *Hot Press* reported that "you couldn't go to the concerts without learning about Amnesty. At every venue, there were tables set up with literature, and postcards to six governments, urging the release of the six prisoners who had been 'adopted' for special attention during the tour."[61] By the end of the Conspiracy of Hope Tour, 60 percent of Americans had heard of Amnesty International. From their next album on, U2 would publicize the organization on the inside sleeve of their jackets. They also talked about political prisoners at hundreds of shows, using personal stories to draw out the emotional side of politics as only U2 could. The Edge even credited the tour with getting Nigerian musician Fela Kuti released from jail.[62]

Perhaps most meaningfully, the tour nearly tripled the U.S. membership of Amnesty International.[63] U2 were conscious of U.S. fears of

Figure 2.2.   Bono, Bryan Adams, and Sting at the Los Angeles concert of the Amnesty International Conspiracy of Hope Tour, June 6, 1986. *REX USA*

anything smacking of protest, especially during the Cold War. As Adam recalled, "The aim of the tour was to make Amnesty a bit clearer in the minds of the American public. A lot of Americans see Amnesty as a communist organisation. But they don't just strive to free people being imprisoned by pro-American regimes. They are active all over the world and the tour tries to emphasize that."[64] The tour got young Americans directly involved in Amnesty's core activity, writing letters to governments imprisoning prisoners of conscience. "All over America," Bono said the following year, "they had set up these clubs where they listen to U2 records and actually write cards for Amnesty. If you can inspire something on that small scale, that's everything I could ask for."[65] According to Dunphy, the tour demonstrated that "Reagan's America still had a conscience."[66]

"I think it was recognized that there was a new mood amongst music fans to effect change in the world," Bono later recalled, "and our audience was at the forefront of that. Whether it was Live Aid, the antiapartheid movement or Amnesty International, music was now seen as a unifying force, a kind of glue to make a new political constituency."

It was true, he added, that U2 pursued "very clear, achievable goals—some would say easy targets. Some would say we were avoiding the hard fights. But, in 1985, who could tell apartheid would fall? Who could predict that Amnesty International could be so effective? It is true that we weren't narrow, we were broad; that was our power, and it still is."[67]

Almost as soon as the Conspiracy of Hope Tour ended, in mid-July 1986 Bono and Ali flew to Central America to witness another great tragedy of the decade: proxy wars waged by the Reagan government against the socialist regime in Nicaragua and the socialist insurgency in next-door El Salvador. Again, what brought U2 to activism was the work of other activists. Through Chilean artist René Castro, whose life has been saved by Amnesty International, Bono visited the legendary Glide Memorial United Methodist Church in San Francisco and heard about Central American Mission Partners, a human rights and development group that organized the Hewsons' trip. Bono also got involved in financing communes before his trip. Bono and Ali spent about a week in Nicaragua, where they heard President Daniel Ortega give a speech and met with Minister of Culture Ernesto Cardenal, who told them that his Sandinista revolution was inspired by the Irish uprising of 1916. Bono and Ali traveled another four or five days in El Salvador, visiting the U.S. embassy and a group of women whose children were killed by the right-wing government or "disappeared."[68]

In Central America's streets and country roads, said Bono, "we saw the blight that was the Bush-Reagan era."[69] Empty supermarket shelves, bodies thrown from vehicles, others dead on the side of the road, terrorized peasants, and fusillades that opened up at a moment's notice—Bono and Ali were caught up in one in El Salvador—such was the daily reality in 1980s Central America. "It's just very sad to see the stranglehold America has on Central America in practice," he remarked a few years later. "It seemed like years, the weeks I spent there. It just makes Amnesty International seem like a very good idea."[70] "There is no question in my mind that the people of America through their taxes are paying for the equipment that is used to torture people in El Salvador," he told *Propaganda*, U2's own magazine.[71]

Bono's political ideas were becoming clearer. The successful revolution in Nicaragua was, for Bono, "a coming together of many of my interests: Christianity, social justice, artists in power."[72] His vision of a Christianity that cares for the poor—embodied by liberation theology priests—was living in Central America. The counterexample was the so-called Christian Right of Reagan's America, which was oblivious to if not complicit in the massacres. Bono explicitly compared the two:

> There is a radical side to Christianity that I am attracted to. And I think without a commitment to social justice, it is empty. Are they putting money in AIDS research? Are they investing in hospitals so the lame can walk? So the blind can see? Is there a commitment to the poorly fed? Why are people left on the side of the road in the US? Why, in the West, do we spend so much money on extending the arms race instead of wiping out malaria, which could be eradicated given 10 minutes' worth of the world's arms budget? To me, we are living in the most un-Christian times.[73]

Twenty years later, Bono noted the "great irony for me" of collaborating on AIDS issues with some of the same conservatives who waged war on Nicaragua in the 1980s.[74]

Bono also saw liberation theologians, whom he visited in Nicaragua, as "too material" in their concerns. Reflecting his experience with the IRA, he observed, "I did not like the romanticization of the revolution that I found [in Nicaragua]. Because I think there is no glory in dying a bloody death."[75] Bono was partly cautious for political reasons. Fans were unaware that he considered himself a Sandinista sympathizer, and if Bono's associations were widely known, they may have been detrimental to his image as an enemy of war.[76]

Altogether, Central America helped Bono refine his stance on violence:

> The difference between the Sandinistas and the Provisional IRA was that the Sandinistas represented a majority of their country. I was just trying to figure out: was there any reason to take up arms? On the one hand, you had Martin Luther King saying "Never," Gandhi saying "Never," Jesus Christ, both their inspirations in this saying "Never." On the other hand, here were the Sandinistas saying "We have to look after the poor, we have to defend the poor." . . . In the end, ideas are not worth as much as people. . . . Marxism-Leninism was an extraordinary idea to lead mankind out of its squalor. It was a dangerous idea that almost made sense.[77]

One of the band's most stalwart friends of the following decade, writer Salman Rushdie, happened to be in Nicaragua at the same time. He never crossed paths with the Hewsons, but they heard of each other at the time. Bono later read Rushdie's book *The Jaguar Smile*, about Nicaragua, and invited him to a U2 concert.[78]

As he often did, Bono struggled to translate politics and activism into musical emotion. "They were bad times," he recalled. "I described what I had been through, what I had seen, some of the stories of the people I had met."[79] With "dismantling the mythology of America" as an objective, Bono instructed The Edge to "put El Salvador through your amplifier."[80]

The result was "Bullet the Blue Sky." The song appeared on *The Joshua Tree*, U2's greatest album commercially—and, some would argue, artistically—and a live version was a highlight of *Rattle and Hum* and its companion documentary, which did well commercially but less so with critics. The popularity of the albums and the years of touring around them allowed U2 not only to reach the mainstream but also to help define it—in activism as well as in music. Within months, the band topped albums and singles charts, made the cover of *Time* and (again) *Rolling Stone*, and became the top-grossing live act in the United States.

U2's views could now reach audiences in the tens of millions, and those views were as urgent as ever. *The Joshua Tree*'s themes—destructive U.S. foreign policies, Irish labor problems, heroin, the "disappeared," and spiritual and moral longing—reflected the band's growing identity as activists. And while lyrics were most concerned with the United States, they also alluded to Argentina, Chile, Ethiopia, Wales, New Zealand, El Salvador, and of course Dublin.[81]

Touring in and writing about the United States in the late 1980s profoundly dimmed the band's mood. The Edge warned that "we're entering into a whole new era here, a frightening new era." "The real world is far more dark, far more dangerous," agreed Bono. "It scares me a lot, this kind of 'let's forget the 60s' mentality, the new fascism, the new conservatism. But America's always been the best and worst rolled into one, and it's going to be very interesting to see how it goes in the next couple of years. I'm a little fearful, but it's as bad in Europe. . . . If you think about the years that went before and the years that have come after, it's the 60s that are weird, not the 70s, not the 80s."[82]

A half decade of Reagan conservatism was taking its toll, and The Edge noticed. "It's a very different America from the one we've seen over the last couple of years. People were so behind everything Ronald Reagan stood for but now I think when we go back, we'll be seeing a broken country in a sense. Either that or people refusing to look—which is a more frightening prospect. I've been talking to some Americans since Irangate [the Iran-Contra scandal]. People's faith in the Administration, and therefore their faith in politics generally, shattered." Bono again saw conservatism as more cyclical: "There's a right-wing vein running through America at the moment and it's made of steel and with all the will in the world, it seems almost impossible to break or bend that it lies dormant for maybe a few years and it comes out with its cold steely grip on America." He lay some of the blame at the feet of Americans' ingenuousness, which he admired. "It's their openness that leads them to trust a man as dangerous as Ronald Reagan. They want to believe he's a good guy. They want to believe that he's in the cavalry, coming to rescue America's reputation after the Seventies. But he was only an actor. It was only a movie. I think the picture's ended now and Americans are leaving the cinema feeling a little down in the mouth."[83]

Band members noted the rampant inequality and social scourges that resulted from Reagan-era selfishness. "There's this humongous wealth—y' know every convertible is red and it's driven by a blonde-haired woman," noted Adam. "And you have this street-life of massive homelessness.

For a start, the mental patients they don't keep, you have this serious problem where if people are mentally sick and poor, there's no welfare, there's no nothing. So they live in these cheap hotels, they rent a room."

"In certain areas," added The Edge, "it's like Beirut. There's probably 2 to 3 killings in L.A. every day, where the different districts of the ghetto areas are divided and controlled by the different gangs, the Crips and the Bloods, and so on." "Fear is running America at the moment," Adam declared, "which leads to the whole arms issue. Everyone is carrying guns—you have ghettoes where the gangs have superior fire-power to the police. . . . There just doesn't seem to be any way they can close that door, because if you're poor in America you don't have anything."[84]

"I think it's wrong for pop-stars to be politicians," said Bono when *The Joshua Tree* came out, partly walking back the comments of his band. "You're put in a position where, because you have made music that means something to people, your politics or point of view is given far too much importance. What comes to mind is Elvis Presley who meets with [President Richard] Nixon and he's made an anti-drug marshall—and the man is loaded, out of his brains, with the badge on." In order not to be ridiculed as modern Elvises, when U2 did speak on politics, especially non-Irish politics, they were increasingly careful. "I don't feel liberal at all and I don't think anyone who knows me would call me liberal," Bono stated in the same interview. "I'm trying to come to terms with global ideas like Live Aid, Artists Against Apartheid, Amnesty International and the 'Conspiracy of Hope' tour. These ideas are great ideas. . . . Yet, for me, the future lies in small scale activity. For instance, commitment to a community, like U2 are committed to Dublin, commitment to the people in your place of work, commitment to relationships and the ones you love."[85]

An opportunity for small-scale activism arose during U2's 1987 U.S. tour, when Republican governor Evan Mecham of Arizona rescinded a state holiday in honor of Martin Luther King Jr. U2 learned that Stevie Wonder and the Doobie Brothers had canceled Arizona dates in protest. Simultaneously, Bono was allegedly receiving death threats, one of which the Federal Bureau of Investigation took seriously since a racist was promising to shoot Bono if he sang his ode to King, "Pride (In the Name of Love)":

I do remember actually, in the middle of Pride, thinking, for a second, "Gosh! What if somebody was organized, or in the rafters of the building or somebody here and there just had a handgun?" I just closed my eyes and I sang the middle verse, with my eyes closed, trying to concentrate and forget about this ugliness and just keep close to the beauty that's suggested in the song. I looked up, at the end of that verse, and Adam was standing in front of me. It was one of those moments where you know what it means to be in a band. [86]

U2 chose not to cancel its planned Arizona concert at Sun Devil Stadium in December but instead to stir controversy. [87] They met with and made a donation to the Mecham Watchdog Committee, an effort to recall the governor. The band also called Mecham's rescission "an embarrassment to the people of Arizona. We condemn his actions and views as an insult to a great spiritual leader. We urge all forward thinking Arizonians to support the campaign to recall Governor Mecham." U2 failed in the short term, but in 1992, the voters of Arizona did implement the King holiday through a ballot initiative. [88]

It was clear from this episode, however, that U2 still preferred to stay away from political campaigns, wading in only when compelled by public opinion.

In Chile, Bono again taunted authorities from the stage, again to mixed results. While the Augusto Pinochet dictatorship was still in power, U2 played their dirge about victims of his and other regimes, "Mothers of the Disappeared":

> We asked for the show to be televised that night. . . . I brought the *madres* [mothers] out on the stage, and they said the names of the missing children into the microphone. Then I spoke to Pinochet as if he was there, as if he was watching television . . . : "Mister Pinochet, God will be your judge, but at the very least, tell these women where the bones of their children are buried." . . . And this crowd divided quickly into two halves. One half cheered, and one half booed, because there are still mixed feelings about what went on. I thought: "Wow! This is not all just people who are on our side. They don't agree with us." [89]

There were several other benefits in the 1980s, including a Carolina Concert for Children in Chapel Hill, North Carolina, in 1983; a 1988 "Smile Jamaica" concert for victims of Hurricane Gilbert; and an International Very Special Arts Festival to celebrate disabled artists in 1989.[90] U2 also covered Darlene Love's "Christmas (Baby, Please Come Home)" for the hugely successful 1987 album *A Very Special Christmas* to help fund the Special Olympics. The following year, they contributed Woody Guthrie's searing "Jesus Christ" to a Smithsonian Institution project. And work continued for Amnesty International and the environmental organization Greenpeace. These were almost always prudent causes with little opposition. Bono admitted in 1989 "that we are attracted to issues that unify people rather than divide them." He did, however, begin to speak out about AIDS discrimination, homophobia, and abortion, and in 1990 the band released the single "Night and Day" to raise money for AIDS charities.[91]

* * *

"Over the past few years, rock & roll has gone a long way toward establishing itself as a force for good in the world," wrote *Rolling Stone* in 1987, "and U2 has been at the forefront of the artists who have contributed to that movement. The band's 1983 LP *War* helped restore social consciousness to rock, and its galvanizing performances at Live Aid and during Amnesty International's six-concert Conspiracy of Hope tour defined the dual spirit of moral purpose and fervent celebration."[92]

That same year, Irish writer John Waters, a critic of the Self Aid concert, adopted a more conciliatory attitude. "We expect too much of U2," he wrote. "They cannot abolish unemployment, renew the city centre, feed the poor or make the Hot House Flowers a hit band. . . . Their great strength has been the open and honest expression of the things that concerned them personally." Yet Waters also admired "their potential as a force for political good. So far that potential has been under-realized."[93]

U2 indeed spent the 1980s finding themselves in the world. They went from an Irish hit to a global phenomenon, and the world's causes became theirs. They were not socialists but still fierce critics of runaway capitalism. They mostly took on "safe" liberal causes but were effective at making them acceptable to the mainstream. And throughout it all, they infused their messages with calls for justice, freedom, and generosity in what they identified as an age where all these virtues were lacking.

3

ZOOROPA, 1990–1998

We're just as serious about what we do now. We're just pretending not to be.—Bono[1]

In the 1990s, U2 experimented not only with a new image and new music but also with an enhanced activism. It may have appeared in the first years of the Zoo TV extravaganza that the band had given up changing the world. But U2 was recharging its batteries for a deeper dive. Bono and the gang now moved beyond the benefit concerts and onstage speeches and involved themselves in direct action—putting their bodies on the line, or at least trying to, and getting more involved in political campaigns. Such deepening involvement actually mirrored their musical boldness during the decade, as did the increasing globalization of both.

U2's breaking of boundaries sprang from the sense of disorder that pervaded the 1990s. The world dragged U2 deeper into activism. The 1980s were marked by war and human rights violations, but both were often results of the "order" visited on the world by the conservative age, whether led by U.S. President Ronald Reagan, British Prime Minister Margaret Thatcher, or the Soviets. Ironically, the victory of capitalism over communism and the acceleration of globalization unleashed historical forces that shook established hierarchies, the first among these in Europe.

So while U2's 1980s focused largely on activism in the United States, their 1990s would bring them back closer to home. "Europe is very ordered and civilized," Adam had said in 1987, "but America is just this weird fucking jungle."[2] In the 1990s, Europe was the jungle—Zooropa—

and U2 found itself in the middle of it. "You're drawn to where the heat is," Bono explained in the early 1990s. "And in the late 80s it was America. Right now it's Europe."[3]

* * *

The end of the Cold War and the creation of the European Union were but symptoms of a more fundamental takeover of Western societies by market forces and ethnic and religious strife that signaled the globalization of selfishness. War was breaking out in the former Yugoslavia. Fascism was returning to Europe. Such abrupt historical change unsettled modern society. Postmodern culture grew "depthless," as scholars of globalization observed, "anchored neither in the co-ordinates of time and place." Ubiquitous shopping malls, fast-food restaurants, and airport terminals were increasingly homogeneous "non-places."[4] Partly in response to this dislocation and rootlessness, communities and individuals in them began to lose their sense of place and uniqueness. It was no surprise that, after stepping off the last flight into East Germany before the country ceased to exist, U2 stumbled into a procommunist march.[5] Confusion reigned. Orthodoxies were crumbling. Activism would have to be reimagined.

U2 best expressed these disconnects with their song "Zooropa," which writer Robert Vagacs referred to as "the anti-matter of 'Where the Streets Have No Name.'"[6] The song opened with a cacophony of background noises, followed by advertising slogans from Audi, Toshiba, United Airlines, Colgate, and many others, then to a breakdown of the postmodern condition, where questions abounded without answers and all sense of direction was lost ("And I have no compass/And I have no map . . . And I have no religion/And I don't know what's what/And I don't know the limit/The limit of what we've got").

Out of this chaos, some sought to reconstruct the local, to reimagine community relationships. According to one philosopher, U2 addressed "postmodern conundrums: What happens to personal integrality, faith, and purposeful moral action in a pervasively ironic and detached postmodern culture? How does an individual commit to heroic ideas and action if identity is so elusive, shallow, and fragmented? If society so thoroughly rejects the authority of religious and political ideologies and if the media environment sanctions ironic couch potato criticism as a valid form of political engagement, how can one help to improve society and the world?"[7]

Bono's response, it seems, was to emphasize the human—imagination and humor: "Uncertainty can be a guiding light," "Get your head out of the mud baby," and "She's gonna dream up the world she wants to live in" were "Zooropa's" hopeful final thoughts. As Scott Calhoun wrote of the 1990s, "Not only was U2 producing culture but its product was a delicious, intelligent critique of the inherent limitations of a consumer-centric approach to life and the 'stuff' we turn to for satisfaction."[8]

U2, therefore, were still seeking to root themselves in an increasingly disjointed world. As John Waters explained in 1994, "This cosmopolitan form of life made possible by globalising technology and the supra-national institutions of the EU can be an alienated existence where people look through one another without seeing each other, talk without communicating, are pushed together without touching or feeling—a world where people are made so close but yet far away from one another."[9]

U2 chose to counter alienation by delving into alienation, in large part as a response to critics of their 1980s image. Bono warned early against what John Lennon called the wariness of being "benefited to death," but it happened anyway. In the 1980s, U2 became the biggest band in the world with the loudest microphone, and the backlash followed.

The seriousness with which U2 took its consciousness-raising efforts in the late 1980s clashed with the machinery of fame in the Western world—which builds up stars in order to break them down. The iconic images the band projected of themselves as desert-dwelling ascetics also did them no favors. They were millionaires dressing like paupers, perceived as preachy and pompous. The Irish press, as *Musician* noted, especially "questioned the efficacy, if not the good intentions, of U2's concern for the world's underprivileged." U2 bristled at the accusation of poor intentions but otherwise could not point to concrete results of its activism apart from the increase in Amnesty International's membership after U2 toured for the human rights organization.[10] *The New Yorker* added insult to injury, arguing that "U2's rage has a relentless, monolithic quality that can become frightening in its lack of humor."[11]

"Being the Batman and Robin of rock & roll has its disadvantages," The Edge responded, with, ironically, the band's typical brand of humor.[12] The other side, too, had jokes: "How many members of U2 does it take to change a light bulb? Just one: Bono holds the light bulb and the world revolves around him."[13]

Larger cultural forces were also at work. One scholar noted the late-century "paradigm shift in Western culture from modernism and its reliance on human reason to post-modernism and its claim that truth can't be attained." Such a shift "made legalism and moral absolutes a hard-sell." Having spent a decade giving concerts at which the moral absolutes were as clear as in a church, how would U2 adjust to this increasingly cynical world?[14]

After taking a break from exhausting tours that nearly broke up the band in the 1980s, in October 1990 U2 regrouped tentatively at Hansa Studios in Berlin. Bono's idea was to emulate the reunification process of East and West Germany and bring back U2 as a better band, more confident in its identity.[15]

The new Germany's capital and its Zoo Station seemed to embody the runaway capitalism of the early 1990s, Bono later recalled. "Berlin was *disappearing by the second*. It was being *bought by the yard*. Every businessman, every hooker as a result, in Europe seemed to be there. It was like goldrush. It was a very interesting energy to be around."[16] U2 had already expressed interest in political change on the continent. Their early hit "New Year's Day" sympathized with Poland's plight. New Year's Eve in 1989 saw the BBC broadcast a U2 concert in Dublin to Eastern Europe and the Soviet Union as a tribute to democratic reforms.[17]

In the 1990s, however, sincere tributes were passé. Unable to shake their do-gooder, holier-than-thou image, U2 chose to embrace the irony that was becoming the dominant tone of the 1990s.

The tours that followed the release of *Achtung Baby* (1991) were expensive, media-saturated spectacles that assaulted the senses with absurdity, pranks, and crass taste. U2 shows, previously stripped-down affairs, now moved lightning fast from one image or phrase to another in mimicry of the dominant cultural format of the age, cable television, the ultimate medium of alienation.[18] Bono, The Edge, Larry, and Adam embraced the opposite image of the band in the 1980s, now portraying themselves as phony, sexy, and materialistic.

"We had to get through to the MTV generation," Adam explained.[19] But, in keeping with his new image, Bono said of U2 fans, "If they don't get it, I don't give a fuck."[20]

Yet Bono was, as he admitted, "just looking for a new way to express old idealism." "As you get older, your idea of good guys and bad guys changes as we moved from the 80s to the 90s. I stopped throwing rocks at the obvious symbols of power and the abuse of it. I started throwing rocks at my own hypocrisy."[21]

The band remained committed to some of the same organizations, but, as Bono explained, "The first duty of any rock'n'roll band is not to be boring so I don't want to be *boring* about our involvement with Greenpeace or Amnesty International or anything else."[22] And despite the on-stage antics, the band's determination to tackle social ills survived. "We are still serious," Bono reassured Waters. "Painfully serious. Obsessively, boringly serious about all the questions that we were so earnest about in the 80s. It's just that we've gotten better at disguising that, at packaging that."[23]

U2 was thus moving away from an activism of protest and resistance to one of softening up the enemy so as to change conditions from the inside. After three years of touring, Bono thought his band had achieved their goal "to describe the age and challenge it." "We were confirmed about our instincts that the idea of counterculture, the way it used to be in the sixties, that number is up. And I'm interested in these more Asian ideas, which we playfully call judo, that you use the energy of what's going against you—and by that I just mean popular culture, commerce, science—to defend yourself. Rather than resistance, in the hippie or punk sense of the word, you try to walk through it rather than walk away from it."[24]

The idea of placing giant television images on U2's stages was a response to the 1991 Persian Gulf War, the first to be broadcast on satellite television. While recording *Achtung Baby*, Bono and The Edge, like millions, witnessed the absurdity of a war in which U.S. pilots dropped precision bombs and surveyed the damage on a video screen, just like a game—a game that killed hundreds of thousands. When one pilot remarked, "It's so realistic," the singer and guitarist looked at each other. They sensed a dangerous desensitization of humanity.[25]

Once in a while, therefore, U2 could not help but get involved in world affairs. In 1995, Bono walked up to the microphone at the MTV Europe Awards just as France was carrying out nuclear bomb tests in the South Pacific and blurted, "What a city. What a night. What a crowd! What a bomb! What a mistake! What a wanker you have for President!

What are you gonna do about it?"[26] It was a glimmer of the righteous Bono of the 1980s but with a soupçon of naughtiness.

In 1992, the band took a cue from activist organizations and put its bodies on the line in a protest. Larry, who rarely spoke to the media, especially about politics, explained the reasoning:

> After we did Amnesty International and Live Aid and a lot of benefit concerts, Bono and I sat down and talked about how we were going to approach the future. We came to the conclusion that maybe the best to do was leave Amnesty—continue to support them, obviously, but doing more concerts may be a mistake for now—and let's do something for Greenpeace. We've donated to them for a long time, we've done gigs with them, but we've never actually been involved in an action. When this came up, it was an opportunity.[27]

In June 1992, U2 first headlined a protest concert against British Nuclear Fuels Limited's plans for a thermal oxide reprocessing plant at the Sellafield nuclear processing plant, located across the Irish Sea from Ireland. After traveling for hours after the show, in the wee hours of the next day U2 boarded the Greenpeace ship *Solo* to approach the plant by water so as to circumvent a British court order barring demonstrations on Sellafield property. U2 and Greenpeace activists, who thought that the existing plant already bred illness across the sea, made it to the high-water mark, where Sellafield land began.

Here was a seminal moment in U2's direct action. Bono declared his intention to break the court order, but Greenpeace talked him out of it, saying it would lead to London seizing all of the organization's assets. Yet U2 still waded through irradiated water and trudged through irradiated sand to help line up almost two miles of placards reading "React–Stop–Sellafield" and dump barrels of contaminated Irish soil on the ground. Adhering to U2's new jocular image, Bono donned his wraparound "Fly" shades, and the band, wearing white radiation suits and yellow fluorescent life jackets, semaphored H-E-L-P and F-O-A-D for "Fuck Off And Die" (see figure 3.1). At a press conference on the same beach, the band spoke out against plans for Sellafield 2 and Ireland's inaction against it.[28]

The protest was a failure—for a time. Sellafield 2 went online in March 1994. Yet it was shut down several times for safety violations and is due to close in 2018.

Figure 3.1.   The Edge, Larry, Bono, and Adam join Greenpeace in a beach protest in front of the Sellafield nuclear reprocessing plant in Cumbria, United Kingdom, June 1992. *Photofusion/Rex/REX USA*

"I suppose it's a token gesture," admitted Bono in 1992. "We've given one day in a year. It's not much." But he was conscious of the reach of his fame. "Greenpeace have got more publicity in the last week than they have probably got in the whole of the previous year." "[If it means] that people who were interested in the band then become focused on such important issues then it was worth it."[29] One resident of nearby Cumbria, whose daughter Gemma died of leukemia that she believed was leaked by Sellafield, appreciated that "during the concert U2 played one of her favorite songs for Gemma, 'Eternal Flame.' . . . It's a lonely struggle, [but the protest] has enlightened people's views on Sellafield. When the likes of U2 stand up and say that they are fighting it, that's different. They have a big following and a lot more people sat up suddenly and took notice."[30]

Again, too, U2 had a long relationship with Greenpeace. They had given the group rights to use their songs to raise funds, and Greenpeace set up fund-raising tables at every stop on the Zoo TV tour.[31]

Soon after Sellafield came the U.S. presidential election, and U2 found itself involved more directly than they expected. In 1988, the band had refused to endorse Democratic presidential contender Jesse Jackson on the grounds that the band shouldn't meddle in U.S. elections. But in 1992, the relationship that developed with Bill Clinton was more organic. The band and the then governor of Arkansas happened to be staying in the same hotel in Chicago. U2, a few drinks in them, asked the governor's entourage if he could join them, but in vain. The next morning, however, Clinton showed up in a hungover Bono's room, Bono mumbling to The Edge, "Okay, let's see how much of a politician this guy really is." When Clinton saw Bono "elegantly wasted," as journalist Bill Flanagan recalled, he fell over laughing. The two discussed music and then politics, with Larry, ever the cynic, asking Clinton why he'd want to enter a world as corrupt as presidential politics. Clinton gave the most Bono-esque response he could have: "This is going to sound corny. But I do love my country and I do want to help people. I know the system is corrupt, and I don't know if the president can change it. But I know this: no one else can." During his early 1990s tours, Bono often dialed the White House from the stage in an effort to annoy it, in the process inflicting damage on Clinton's opponent, George H. W. Bush. "I wasn't sure if it was something we should be involved in," Larry said. "There were differing opinions in the band about being involved at all, about using George Bush." U2 also lent its support for the Rock the Vote youth registration drive, and after the election Clinton assessed that "that wonderful group U2" played an important role in getting him elected. Bono thought Clinton gave them far too much credit, but the band were nevertheless elated at the Arkansan's election. Adam, Larry, and Paul McGuinness attended the inauguration, and the drummer and bassist combined with Mike Mills and Michael Stipe from REM, calling themselves "Automatic Baby," to perform "One" at MTV's inauguration show.[32]

U2's most involved activism of the 1990s, however, concerned war-torn former Yugoslavia, especially Bosnia, whose capital, Sarajevo, was under siege and badly damaged by the forces of Slobodan Milosevic's Serbia. This Balkan tragedy encompassed the worst of the post–Cold War years in Europe—the ethnic and religious hatred, the resurfacing of fascistic tendencies, and the high-tech ability to commit genocide. The brutal siege of one of Europe's most cherished cities and the images of emaciated Bosnian prisoners in World War II–like concentration camps grabbed the attention of the world and clarified the moral stakes.

In April 1993, Adam went on Irish radio to support Amnesty International's driving food and medicine into Bosnia past a Serbian blockade.

Bono was also involved in the effort. But in May, Europe rejected a U.S. push for an intervention by North Atlantic Treaty Organization (NATO) troops, and the situation deteriorated badly.

In early July, the band's actions moved to a higher level. At this point, the siege of Sarajevo had lasted 20 months. Most of the city was without electricity, reliable water supplies, or enough food. The connection between Bosnia and U2 came from Bill Carter, a San Francisco documentary filmmaker who, after he lost his girlfriend in a car crash, joined an unofficial humanitarian group that delivered food to Sarajevans. As U2 were set to play Verona, Italy, Carter grew convinced that more people needed to know about the horrors of the siege. "So I thought if anyone is going to reach out to give this kind of mental humanitarian help in the name of human rights it would be U2."[33]

Carter wrote to U2 feigning to represent Bosnian television, and the band granted him an interview.[34] He traveled two dangerous days from Sarajevo to Italy with television gear to interview Bono and asked him why the barbarity of war still existed.

"The human heart is very greedy," was Bono's answer. "It seeks many excuses for that. Religion is a convenient one, color is a convenient one. I've been through various different stages in working this out. One must be political at times, but sometimes you have to look beyond that to just the state of the human spirit. I guess that's where I'm at right now. I'm examining my own hypocrisy, I'm examining my own greed. I've stopped even pointing at politicians."

Carter told Bono that sending supplies was "all right, but you're feeding a graveyard." "It's just wholesale murder now," Carter said. "They know no one's coming to the rescue." The exchange brought Bono to tears. Carter then suggested that Bono visit. Bono wanted to go the following week, and the rest of the band agreed. "I think that's a good idea," said Adam. "If you believe in a cause you must be willing to put yourself on the line for that cause." "And," commented journalist Flanagan, "that's about all it takes for Adam Clayton to agree to risk his life."[35]

But, Carter and others warned, playing in a Sarajevo that came under almost daily shelling was simply too perilous for band, crew, and fans. "There's not even any power to play!" implored road manager Dennis Sheehan. "Bono's an extremist and he has done some extreme things, but Sarajevo isn't Central America, Sarajevo isn't Ethiopia."

The band debated their responsibility for direct action. "We came to the conclusions that the duty of the artist is to illustrate contradictions and point a finger at things that are wrong and terrible without the responsibility of having to resolve them," McGuinness explained. "U2's efforts to discuss any humanitarian issue have sometimes been accompanied by a false instinct that U2 is also obliged to resolve that issue."[36]

Yet U2 pressed on. As Carter recalled, U2 wanted to do "something radical. Something to seriously jar people out of their numbness to what's happening in this continent."[37] They settled on the idea of a live satellite linkup by which U2 concert audiences would see Sarajevans interviewed by Bono about the suffering of the besieged and the urgency of European intervention. U2's management company, Principle, signed the checks to get the European Broadcast Union to allow the satellite hookup. Guests included Serbs, Croats, and Muslims; artists, soldiers, and writers; and friends of Carter who would arrange a satellite phone with the news agency Reuters and then take the guests to a dark television station where they would broadcast using battery lights. The topics were dark: organized rape and systematic torture. One group of women, for example, stated, "We would like to hear the music, too, but we only hear the screams of wounded and tortured people and raped women!"[38] Bono apologized for calling them from "our little fantasy world." "We are ashamed to be Europeans tonight," he added.[39] Another time, U2 and Carter linked up families in Europe to loved ones in Sarajevo. The first time the linkup ended, from Marseilles, Carter felt that "surreal is the only word that comes to mind. How does one hang up the phone with fifty thousand people and U2 and walk into a war?"[40]

The atmosphere at the shows was equally surreal, if nowhere near as dangerous. U2 connected Sarajevo to hundreds of thousands of its fans, a captive audience that could not change the channel. Because of the dozen linkups, U2's 1993 shows, meant to be statements of escapism, suddenly screeched to a halt to face the grimmest reality as Carter packed interviewees in his car and drove them—headlights off, at almost 90 miles an hour—through Sarajevo's "Sniper's Alley" as bullets zipped by, some hitting the car.[41]

Some thought the stunt embarrassing, awkward, or exploitative. "The worst night was Wembley Stadium," recalled McGuinness, "when 3 women came up on the screen and said, 'We don't know what we're doing here. This guy dragged us in. You're all having a good time. We're not having a good time. What are you going to do for us?' Bono started to reply but they just cut him off. They said, 'We know you're not going to do anything for us. You're going to go back to a rock show. You're going to forget that we even exist. And we're all going to die.' Right in the middle of a show at Wembley. And the show never really recovered."[42]

But U2 had many defenders, one being Salman Rushdie, the author against whom the Ayatollah Khomeini of Iran issued a death-sentence fatwa, forcing him into hiding until U2 invited him onstage at an August 1993 Wembley show. It was Rushdie's first major public appearance in five years, and he witnessed one of the linkups. "I thought exactly the awkwardness of it, the ill-fittingness, was what made it memorable. I've never been made, in a rock & roll show, to feel the pain of the world before. . . . We live in an age when people want to reinvent a whole bunch of demarcation lines and say, 'If you're a rock band don't step across the line into news coverage. . . .' I think all creative activity, in fact, is a process of *destroying* frontiers."[43]

Larry also justified the Bosnia interviews as "the essence of good rock & roll—it's about confusion on every level. . . . On one hand, you can have Sarajevo, which is real, and then you have to continue on with the show. I mean, even for us, after the Sarajevo linkups we did, carrying on the show was incredibly difficult. People took it in different ways. People took it as 'How can you have irony and then be serious?' but that is the point." "That's TV!" interjected Bono.[44]

U2 decided to put an end to the linkups after four shows in London because, according to Flanagan, "by coincidence or indirect effect, Sarajevo has gone from being virtually unmentioned in the press three weeks earlier to dominating the front pages of the British papers every day."[45]

U2's commitment to Sarajevo continued after the tour. Bono funded a documentary by Carter called "Miss Sarajevo" and, by writing a recommendation, got its star to be admitted to a U.S. university. Bono had suggested the title to Carter and promised to write a song with the same name for it. "Miss Sarajevo," recorded with Luciano Pavarotti and released in 1995, stands as arguably U2's most moving song, inspired by the "Miss Besieged Sarajevo" beauty contest of 1993.[46] In late 1995, Bono and Ali flew into the city for the first time aboard a UN aid flight (see figure 3.2).[47]

U2's closure on Sarajevo came on September 23, 1997, when the war was over and the band insisted that they play the city. People cheered as

Figure 3.2.   Bono visiting the ruins of the Sarajevo library on December 31, 1995.
AP Photo/Santiago Lyon

U2's trucks drove toward the battered stadium, which had served as a morgue during the war but which NATO peacekeepers now protected. Larry's hotel room walls were embedded with mortar shrapnel, and parts of the floor were missing. The band discussed Irish-Bosnian similarities with the president of Bosnia-Herzegovina, and with the Bosnian ambassador they visited the sites of atrocities and battles. During the show, with Bono's voice hoarse from laryngitis, U2 celebrated the off-duty peacekeepers present—and even more so the people themselves for surviving the ordeal. The band gave the proceeds of the show to a local hospital rebuilding program. "Today was the day the siege of Sarajevo ended," proclaimed an editorial the following day.[48]

As in the 1980s, the U2 community also kept busy in the 1990s with dozens of consciousness- or fund-raising appearances. In February 1991, U2 paid a £500 fine for the Irish Family Planning Association, which illegally sold condoms in Dublin, simultaneously drumming up press for the organization. In April–May 1993, Ali and Dreamchaser Productions went to Chernobyl, Russia, to film *Black Wind, White Land*, a documentary about the effects of the 1986 nuclear disaster there. In August, U2's three shows in Ireland benefited seven charities.[49] Later that year, Bono covered Lou Reed's "Perfect Day" for the BBC's Children in Need campaign.[50] In 1994, U2 donated a song to Greenpeace's *Alternative NRG* album. In 1996, another compilation album came out, this time in Australia and including a U2 song for the people of East Timor fighting for independence from Indonesia.[51] In June 1997, the band appeared at the Tibetan Freedom Concert in New York City.[52] The 1990s also saw U2 playing Poland, Central America, South America, and South Africa for the first time.

Bono even donated a sketch of his penis to an auction for Romanian orphans. He had been asked to contribute his "favorite childhood toy."[53]

Up to the 1990s, U2 had made every effort not to align itself explicitly with a political campaign or party. Their dalliance with Clinton was somewhat accidental. The pull of politics again appeared in 1998, when on April 10, after years of negotiation, Northern Ireland's Unionists (who wanted to continue a political union with Great Britain) and Nationalists (who wanted independence) signed the Good Friday Agreement, which set up a power-sharing cabinet. Seeing the parties compromise and choose peace was also the fulfillment of a U2 dream from the *War* years. The signatories won the Nobel Peace Prize that year, and The Edge and Paul McGuinness attended the ceremony.

For the third time in the 1990s—after Sellafield and Bosnia—U2's activism went beyond consciousness raising and engaged in direct action. Referenda to put the Good Friday Agreement into effect were set for May 22 in both the Republic of Ireland and Northern Ireland. Encouragement to vote "Yes" came from statesmen such as President Clinton and South Africa's Nelson Mandela. Yet some Nationalist campaigners were afraid of a close vote, so they invited U2 to drum up support at a rock concert in Belfast on May 19. With The Edge and Adam raised as Protestants, Larry a Catholic, and Bono mixed, U2 considered themselves living examples of Irish unity. They shared the stage with a younger act from Northern Ireland and played the Waterfront Hall, a venue shared by both communities.[54]

From the stage, Bono called up Unionist David Trimble and Nationalist John Hume and raised their arms skyward to the roar of the crowd (see figure 3.3). "When Bono brought John Hume and David Trimble together it was very striking," recalled former taoiseach Garret Fitzgerald. "That was a very dramatic moment. But Bono has that strong commitment to issues in Northern Ireland and to other issues more globally. And he has used his considerable influence, derived from his popularity, very constructively."[55] Bono called the gig "the greatest honor of my life." "People tell me that rock concert and that staged photograph pushed the people into ratifying the peace agreement. I'd like to think that's true."[56]

Figure 3.3.   Bono with David Trimble and John Hume in Belfast in support of voting "Yes" on the Good Friday Agreement, 1998. *Martin McCullough/REX USA*

It probably wasn't. Here, critics such as Harry Browne accurately deflated Bono's suggestion that U2 saved the referendum. The polls were never close. The "Yes" vote easily won 95 percent in Ireland and even 71 percent in Northern Ireland. Because of the result, however, Browne unfairly labeled Bono "a conventional-thinking opportunist who could spot the shortest distance between himself and some great global publicity."[57] Another Irish reporter was even more scathing, saying Bono "carefully picks and chooses his 'issues.' He has, for example shamelessly turned a blind eye for years to the continuing existence of British-controlled and funded death squads murdering his fellow countrymen and women. And when he has spoken about war in Ireland, he has invariably mouthed the words of the oppressor against the oppressed. Like many others, he appears ashamed to be Irish."[58]

During the pre-vote show, Bono had argued that "to vote no is to play into the hands of the extremists who've had their day. Their day is over as far as we're concerned. We're on to the next century here."[59] Yet the agreement was not a harbinger of peace. Some were skeptical that the signers were in fact able to control the violence, which might spring up no matter what. On August 15, not yet three months after the referendum, a dissident group called the Real IRA detonated a car bomb in Omagh that killed 29 and injured over 300, the worst terrorist attack in the history of Northern Ireland. "It was one of the lowest days in my life," recalled Bono. "Maybe because we felt we had a stake in the peace process, I could not comprehend how people could do something like that. The closest I ever came to a crisis of faith happened after that."[60]

* * *

The 1990s had indeed been difficult for the faithful. The Cold War had given way to insecurity, war, ethnic cleansing, genocide, and rising income inequality. Yet the decade also brought an unprecedented number out of poverty, and its last years saw a wild run-up in Internet-related stocks that showered many with unimagined wealth. U2 were among them. They had spent the early 1980s in relative income insecurity, reinvesting earnings into the band. Only after touring for *Unforgettable Fire* and the 25 million copies of *The Joshua Tree* were they wealthy, and even then the ZooTV tour almost bankrupted them. Many may have wondered if their flashy early 1990s image may have been a surrender to wealth and complacency. It turned out to be the opposite. The band were in a period of transition from protest to direct action, and Bono was even farther ahead, his thoughts already busy with "the next century."

4

BONO, SUPERSTAR LOBBYIST, 1999–2005

I'm tired of dreaming. I'm into doing at the moment.—Bono [1]

In the early years of the twenty-first century, Bono largely struck out on his own to become arguably the globe's preeminent activist. It was an unprecedented, remarkable odyssey. Supported but not accompanied by the rest of the band, Bono made a qualitative jump from consciousness raising and direct action to getting legislation passed that would unlock billions of dollars toward the causes he now placed front and center—debt reduction, AIDS prevention and treatment, ethical trade agreements, and poverty in Africa. In short, Bono became what the band often mocked in previous decades—a politician. In 1988, The Edge had joked that "it gets tough, you know, running Amnesty International, organizing summits between superpowers." [2] Now his bandmate was a spokesperson for several Amnesty-like nongovernmental organizations (NGOs) and met with global leaders at summits several times a year. He had become an insider. An "us against the system" attitude, Bono conceded, had become "anachronistic." [3]

In so doing, Bono increasingly separated his art from his activism, putting his own spin on one of the axioms of politics. "U2 is about the impossible. Politics is the art of the possible. They're very different and I'm resigned to it now." Paraphrasing Gandhi, he explained, "When you sing, you make people vulnerable to change in their lives. You make yourself vulnerable to change in your life. But in the end, you've got to become the change you want to see in the world." [4]

* * *

The fact that Bono and his truly global organizations realized unparalleled change in the world, however, reflected deep and sometimes worrisome trends. One was the rising inequality in the world, where a billion or so lived in abject poverty for what Bono and others perceived to be purely political reasons.[5]

Another was the fact that governments no longer felt a responsibility to care for the poor in their country or other countries. "As the US got richer in the 80s and 90s and reached unimaginable prosperity," Bono explained as an example, "it gave less and less per capita to the trouble spots in the world."[6] If rich governments did commit funds for poverty reduction, it was largely after being lobbied hard by Bono and like-minded activists.

A third trend was the growing power of transnational civil society, whose organizations had increased in number and budgets since the 1970s in inverse relation to the diminishing weight of governments. NGOs, especially, were central to this civil society, and those operating internationally numbered over 40,000 in 2014, 10 times more than in 1980. While the growth of NGOs could certainly be morally uplifting and effective, it also signaled a "postdemocratic" age, when institutions of democracy still existed but real policy was often formulated by elites unaccountable to voters, no matter what their intentions.[7]

A fourth trend was the domination of mass image-driven media over small-scale printed press, a change that depended partly on the value of celebrity. (Celebrities were also no longer under the studio system, allowing them more freedom of action, including in their philanthropy.) Television and the Internet, the two dominant forms of mass media, also accelerated the formation of a global conscience because of their ability to communicate immediately images of faraway suffering and to allow networking and organization across barriers of citizenship, race, religion, and geography.[8]

A fifth and final trend was the persistence of racism and other forms of discrimination as globalization confronted privileged Europeans and U.S. citizens with their neglect of the suffering of darker-skinned peoples. The U2 frontman called equality "a great tradition. . . . Equality is an idea that was first really expressed by the Jews when God told them that everyone was equal in His eyes. . . . After a while, people accepted that, though not easily. Rich and poor were equal in God's eyes. But not blacks! . . . Now most people accept that women, blacks, Irish, and Jews are equal, but only within these borders. I'm not sure we accept that Africans are equal."[9]

Blending his perceptions of most of these trends, Bono explained, "What is going on in Africa defies all concepts that we hold to be true: our concept of neighbor, our concept of civilization, our concept of equality, of love. . . . If we really believed the things we say we believe, we would not let 23 million Africans die of AIDS. You can't have the benefits of globalization without some of the responsibilities. We are now next door neighbors through television images, through radio, through the Internet."

"And I promise," he warned, "history will be hard on this moment."[10]

The early 2000s thus saw the rise to prominence of celebrity philanthropists whose intentions could be unimpeachable but whose very existence was a result of the abandonment of the poor by global leaders. In early 2015, one website reported that 3,492 celebrities worked for 2,060 charities.[11] By 2005, private donations to charitable causes were somewhere between $58 billion and $68 billion, about equal or even exceeding "country programmable aid" or aid given by governments.[12] Although coverage of international issues in the United Kingdom had declined since the 1970s, giving rose faster than household income, and giving toward development rose faster than other giving.[13] Overall, stagnating government development budgets intersecting with growing private fortunes created five new groups of givers: "megaphilanthropists," corporations, new bilateral donors such as China, the global public, and celebrities.

Bono was connected to all of these except, arguably, new bilateral donors. He worked with Bill and Melinda Gates, megaphilanthropists whose foundation handled a $30 billion fund and potentially $80 billion more from fellow billionaire Warren Buffett. Bono's Product (RED) project signed agreements with corporations. And he continued to appeal to the broad public for donations, such as when he appeared on *Oprah* in 2002 and on 2007's *American Idol: Idol Gives Back*, which drew 63.5 million viewers.[14]

What set celebrities apart from other activists was their ability to gain access to legislators and others with their hands on the levers of state aid. Actors such as George Clooney, because of their looks and charisma alone, brought immediate media impact to any cause they touched, thus raising their value both to charities and to the politicians who welcomed them into their offices. Actor Natalie Portman, who worked on microfinance, admitted, "I'm not particularly proud that in our country I can get a meeting with a representative more easily than the head of a nonprofit can." As journalist James Traub explained, Bono's often explicit deal with politicians revolved around media: "You give, I say so in public."[15] And when he spoke in public, the media tended to report it. The *New York Times* alone published 404 stories on Bono's activism before 2008.[16] Celebrity activists also more easily recruited other celebrity activists, such as when Brad Pitt invited Bono to his home in 2004 to address celebrities including Tom Hanks, Sean Penn, Julia Roberts, Justin Timberlake, and architect Frank Gehry. Bono also recruited Clooney.[17]

Some celebrities were drawn to activism because they also tended to represent the cosmopolitan impulses of the modern global identity. While the most effective activists were rooted in a community, as U2 were in Dublin (in 2000, they received the Freedom of Dublin award, the mayor appreciating how U2 "continue to live, record and plan their world-class campaigns here" and "support the city's charities and cultural initiatives"), most were also more highly educated than the general population, very well traveled, and, of course, able to devote considerable time and money to activism.[18] (Angelina Jolie reportedly gave one-third of her income to charity.)[19] Because of these backgrounds, celebrity activists valued individual rights and believed in a universal moral order.

Such cosmopolitans contrasted with "locals" or "communitarians," who saw morality as existing only in their communities rather than everywhere.[20] Kofi Annan of the United Nations said that celebrity humanitarians "help instill in young people the values of understanding, solidarity, respect and communication across cultures . . . so that those values come to them naturally for the rest of their lives."[21] The United Nations notably designated actors Nicole Kidman and Don Cheadle, singer Shakira, and footballer David Beckham among around 190 others as UN goodwill ambassadors.

According to scholars, therefore, celebrity activists such as Bono could play crucial roles in global activism. They could bring faraway tragedies closer to home for Western audiences. They could amplify the work of NGOs and others in global civil society. And they could lead through nonconfrontation by persuading political and economic leaders to reorient their resources.[22] A British minister of state for foreign affairs wondered aloud if celebrities were not "a missing link between these detached global elites and mass opinion and mass culture? I think they are obviously filling a vacuum."[23]

Bono first took on the role of superstar lobbyist with the issue of debt forgiveness. Unlike feeding starving Ethiopians or giving hope to war-weary Bosnians, forgiving debts incurred by governments was something that only other governments—and the international financial institutions to which they contributed—could do. And Bono perceived that the poor of Africa had no champion in the halls of power. "I want to have the kind of representation for poor people where they don't have to go up begging for crumbs from our table."[24]

His sympathy for Africa's poor stemmed from his childhood in Ireland. "There is a sort of rage, probably, in me, from childhood, at a certain injustice," he once confided. "I think it's in Irish people." He recounted how the famine in Ireland, just like Africa's debts, was a result of mismanagement rather than single-crop dependency.[25] In 2003, he reminded other Irish that they "should be familiar with the problems facing developing countries; that we were part of that developing world not too long ago . . . the crushing poverty that faces Africa—we are well placed here to understand that."[26] In 2014, he reiterated that "the Irish have an easy solidarity with the world's poorest because, not that long ago, we were them."[27]

The Jubilee 2000 campaign, launched and led by religious groups in the 1990s and involving more than 90 organizations, invoked the injunction from Leviticus 25 to forgive all debts every 50 years. Debt was one of several issues, including trade, that Bono argued were not about charity but rather justice. As Bono explained to Harvard University students, "For every dollar of government aid we sent to developing nations, nine dollars came back in debt service" as a result of Cold War–era Western governments and bankers making careless loans to kleptomaniacal dictators.[28] A generation after Live Aid raised $200 million, Africa spent that much every month on its debt to the West. "It's inefficient, it's barbaric and it's preventing the developing countries from joining the world stage," the singer told the United Nations. "These countries have a lot to offer in terms of growth and new trade but they can't even get to the starting line."[29]

Jubilee first reached out to Bono through Jamie Drummond of Christian Aid, and, by the end of 1998, U2's frontman committed himself to the cause. "We expected that [Bono's involvement] might be concerts and records," recalled Drummond. "But it turned out Bono's a very brilliant political lobbyist."[30]

The first governments targeted were in Europe. In February 1999, Bono both placed an op-ed in *The Guardian* making Jubilee's case and, when accepting a Brit Award for humanitarianism, spontaneously demanded that Western governments "cancel debt repayments by the new millennium." The off-the-cuff speech "was a golden moment," recalled Drummond, because Jubilee got press attention "in a way that we had not managed to do before." A few days later, British Chancellor of the Exchequer Gordon Brown—who had received 500,000 "Cancel the Debt" postcards, including one from his mother—announced that the United Kingdom would wipe clean £50 million in debt at the next G8 Summit and credited Jubilee 2000 for whipping up public opinion. One Jubilee cofounder observed, "It wasn't all down to Bono, of course, but it would have never happened without him."[31]

The U2 community was not done. At the June 1999 G8 Summit in Cologne, Germany, Bono, The Edge, Ali, and 20,000 people demanded debt relief, at one time joining a human chain around the summit facility. Bono and singer Thom Yorke of Radiohead presented German Chancellor Gerhard Schroeder with a 17 million–signature petition. Again the governments responded: the "Cologne Debt Initiative" promised $100 billion in relief out of a total debt of $356 billion.[32] "A hundred billion dollars," reflected Bono in early 2000. "Not bad take-home for a year's work."[33]

In the following years, Bono met also with Canadian, Italian, British, and Russian heads of state as well as with Nelson Mandela and countless others. He became a regular at the World Economic Forum, the World Bank, and the International Monetary Fund (IMF), and his calendar filled up with summits, conferences, fund-raisers, and galas where he hobnobbed with the globe's rich, famous, and powerful (see figure 4.1).[34] When a G8 meeting in Genoa, Italy, was roiled by violence, Bono found himself between his activist and establishment roles: "I don't think violence is ever right," he remarked, "but anger is understandable when facing the obscenity of the ever widening gap of inequality on the planet between the haves and the have nots."[35] For his activism, he appeared on the cover of *Time* three times, once as "Person of the Year" along with Bill and Melinda Gates.[36] In March 2002, he appeared by himself with the headline "Can Bono Save the World?"

On September 9, 1999, Bono spoke to the UN General Assembly in support of NetAid, a campaign to use the Internet to increase awareness of global poverty. The first three people to click on the NetAid website were U.S. President Bill Clinton, British Prime Minister Tony Blair, and Mandela. Two weeks later, Bono, fellow rocker-activist Bob Geldof, and others from Jubilee 2000 met with Pope John Paul II, who endorsed the campaign and appealed to world leaders. Ann Pettifor of Jubilee called September 23 "a day that will go down in history."[37]

Two weeks after that, Bono was back in the New York area for one of three simultaneous NetAid concerts in the United States, England, and Switzerland that were broadcast live on the Internet and on music channels MTV and VH1. One hundred thousand attended the shows, which, through 2.4 million video feeds and 1 billion listeners on television and radio in 132 nations, raised $1.7 million for 15 organizations. Bono and

Figure 4.1.   Bono as global lobbyist. With, left to right, former U.S. President Bill Clinton, Microsoft mogul Bill Gates, South African President Thabo Mbeki, British Prime Minister Tony Blair, and Nigerian President Olusegun Obasanjo at the January 27, 2005, meeting of the World Economic Forum in Davos, Switzerland. *Courtesy of World Economic Forum*

Wyclef Jean also recorded the song "New Day" for the show. The following September, Bono appeared with the Nigerian president at the UN Millennium Summit to give Secretary-General Kofi Annan another petition, signed this time by 21.2 million people in 155 countries.[38] By late 2000, 57 Jubilee networks operated around the world.

The U.S. government was much less aware of Jubilee 2000—even though poor countries owed it $6 billion. It was also stingier than other nations. In 1999, the United States devoted only 0.1 percent of its gross domestic product to development in poor countries.[39] Still, in 2004, Bono lamented that "the U.S. is 'per capita' bottom of the class of twenty OECD [Organization for Economic Cooperation and Development] countries in contributing to the poorest of the poor (no. 15 if you include private philanthropy)."[40]

To get the wheels of government turning in the United States, Bono decided that he "had to go straight to the decision-makers, or at the very least the people who knew those decision makers."[41] Bono set about to infiltrate the lobbying circles in Washington, D.C., to get a bipartisan coalition to pass a $435 million debt relief bill on October 25, 2000. Through "the most extraordinary woman in the world," Eunice Shriver— John F. Kennedy's sister, whom Bono met while working on 1987's *A Very Special Christmas*—Bono met her son Bobby Shriver, who in turn introduced him to his brother-in-law, the actor and Republican operative Arnold Schwarzenegger.

Through "*Ah*-nuld," Bono met a key matchmaker, the Republican congressman John Kasich, chair of the House Budget Committee. Schwarzenegger knew the congressman from holding a bodybuilding contest each year in Columbus in Kasich's Ohio. Kasich had also come away from his travels with the impression that foreigners did not much care for Americans. So he organized meetings between Bono and Republicans Orrin Hatch, Dennis Hastert, and Dick Armey. Bono also met with key Democrats, such as Treasury Secretary Larry Summers, and conservative Republicans, such as Pat Robertson and Jesse Helms, the latter the chair of the Senate Foreign Relations Committee. He made at least 12 trips to Washington and gave countless media interviews to lobby for debt forgiveness. Clinton, who met with Bono early in this process and instructed him on how to get cabinet and congressional approval, recalled how Summers "comes in to my office and says, 'You know, some guy just came in to see me in jeans and a T shirt, and he just had one name, but he sure was smart. Do you know anything about him?'"[42] When signing the bill into law, Clinton cited Bono's "passionate devotion" for bringing together Democrats and Republicans.[43] "I think the place where I had the most impact was the US," Bono admitted.[44]

To be sure, like other celebrity activists, Bono's fame was currency in Washington and other capitals. "The reason why politicians let me in the door, and the reason why people will take my call is because I represent quite a large constituency of people," he explained. "It is a constituency of people from 18 to 30, who are the floating vote."[45] "It is absurd, if not obscene that celebrity is a door that such serious issues need to pass through before politicians take note. But there it is. Jubilee couldn't get into some of these offices but I could."[46]

Bono impressed all in Washington with a trait more rare for a celebrity—mastery of the facts. The singer became a policy wonk. "A lot of celebrities lend their names to something for the moment. But Bono cares," raved Senator Patrick Leahy, who found him "extraordinarily well-prepared. He knows his subject, has a passion for it, and therefore he's far better able to help."[47] Joshua Busby has argued that low expectations are an advantage for celebrity activists, being so easy to surpass.[48]

Bono cared enough to learn from Harvard economist Jeffrey Sachs, who had been preaching that poverty could be eliminated through smarter policies. Sachs himself explained that "celebrities open doors, without question—everyone wants to meet Bono—but the amazing thing about Bono is that they want to meet him again and again because he's not only a celebrity but knows far more about the subject under discussion than the politicians do."[49]

"Everyone I spoke to reiterated how hard Bono has worked on debt cancellation. He is an incredibly knowledgeable guy," noted Noreena Hertz, a distinguished fellow at the University of Cambridge whose writings also influenced Bono. "In conversations with him I can talk at the same level as I would with any economist back at Cambridge. . . . He's not into playing politics to sell records. He is genuinely passionate about it."[50] One staffer in a Treasury meeting recalled that Bono "was referring to a lot of turgid studies—documents on the debt issue, reports for Congress. Everyone was really impressed." "He knew what all the acronyms were," said another, "how the debt flows worked, he knew capital risk." When Bono left the room after a meeting with Summers, the secretary

Figure 4.2. President George W. Bush with Bono discussing AIDS and Africa policies at the White House, October 19, 2005. *Rex/REX USA*

turned to an aide and said, "I think the administration has just had its consciousness raised. This guy's right. We have to fix this."[51]

Bono used his knowledge of the U.S. lobbying process as well, which is all about removing roadblocks before legislation makes it to the floor of a chamber. "Anybody who could put obstacles in our way, we met with them before they could try. Economists, macro-economists, journalists, religious groups, popes, priests, evangelists."[52]

Bono was also persistent. "The most amazing thing was that he kept coming back," Bobby Shriver said of Bono's meetings on Capitol Hill. "He went to one meeting and they were like, 'Nice guy.' He came to a second meeting, and they were like, 'Smart guy.' Then he came to a third meeting and they were like, 'Who is this guy?' By the fourth meeting, they thought, 'We're never gonna get rid of him!' And that has a big influence in Washington. When you keep coming back—and you know your stuff—people start paying attention."[53]

All this lobbying took Bono away from U2's musical career, but the rest of the band understood that he was having an impact far beyond what they could as entertainers trying to raise the consciousness of their fans. "When we heard about Jubilee 2000 we were all on board," said Adam. "We recognized that this was something worth fighting for. We sat down and talked about what we could do as a band but it quickly became apparent that this was a job for one person and the best man for the job was Bono." Larry agreed: "Nobody could argue with what he was doing, it was clearly too important."[54]

Jubilee's achievements should not be overestimated. First, the campaign had the good fortune of not facing an opposing constituency, such as the ones that oppose climate change legislation or the end of agricultural subsidies.[55] Moreover, before Bono ever lobbied it, the White House had already committed to a two-thirds reduction of the debt of the poorest countries through a plan from the World Bank. Bono's work helped bump up the U.S. sum by about $100 million.

Most important, Western leaders were ready to forgive because they knew they would not be repaid anyway. "Forgiveness" was not exactly an aid program but rather an adjustment on accounting ledgers to reflect reality. For the United States, therefore, "canceling" a $6 billion debt cost only about $600 million. And some faulted debt relief for being tied to "conditionalities," or conditions that had to be met with poor countries, such as structural adjustment reforms that might privatize water and electricity services and reduce inflation by cutting back on health and education spending. Harry Browne, a fierce critic of Bono, saw him in this way facilitating global capitalism's domination of Africa by pushing on it the "corporate Washington consensus."[56]

Still, by May 2006, the Jubilee 2000 campaign in Europe and the United States helped 19 nations qualify to have $23.4 billion of their debt canceled through the Heavily Indebted Poor Countries Initiative. The previous year, the World Bank, the IMF, and the African Development Bank committed to writing off all the debts that the poorest countries owed them.[57] Two economists called Jubilee 2000 "by far the most successful industrial-country movement aimed at combating world poverty for many years, perhaps in all recorded history."[58]

Bono's increasingly direct activism also coincided with the terrorist attacks of September 11, 2001, which brought greater seriousness not only to questions of development but also to the entertainment business. In October 2001, Bono observed that "the musical climate has immediately changed. Sugar coated pop doesn't seem to matter much right now. Likewise, the metallic fugue and breast-beating of the hormonal kind. That too has paled."[59]

U2's music had also changed from the electronic, hedonistic feel of their 1990s albums to the bare-bones, earnest sound of 2000's *All That You Can't Leave Behind*. "Just as *Achtung Baby* perfectly reflected the irony obsessed early 90s zeitgeist, *All That You Can't Leave Behind* embodies our renewed taste for the genuine, which has only increased following the events of Sept. 11," wrote Salon.com just a month after the attacks.[60] Bono agreed: "You realize, especially after the events of 9/11, how unimportant it is to be smart. Or worse, smart ass. To be true is all in pop music."[61] To graduates at the University of Pennsylvania in 2004, Bono explained what he perceived as a needed historical shift: "I know idealism is not playing on the radio right now. . . . You don't see it on TV, irony is on heavy rotation, the knowingness, the smirk, the joke. I've tried them all out. Idealism is under siege, beset by materialism, narcissism, and all the other isms of indifference."[62]

"All that you can't leave behind" for Bono meant focusing on "just the essential things. The stuff you can take with you: friendship, laughter. Wisdom, if you've found any. If there is one thing that suffuses the record, it is a sense of mortality, of how and what you treasure in a world where death awaits."[63] Right after September 11, Bono orchestrated an all-star recording of Marvin Gaye's "What's Going On," with proceeds dedicated to 9/11 relief, and on September 21, U2 performed at *A Tribute to Heroes*, a televised concert that raised $150 million for victims of the attacks. U2 particularly connected with U.S. audiences' need for emotional and spiritual healing. At U2's first post-9/11 concert in New York on October 24, the names of police and firefighters who died at Ground Zero scrolled on a screen, as did those of the hijack victims. Listing the names was, to Bono, a way to fight the sense that "these people were stats. . . . Everybody in Madison Square Garden could see somebody they knew or somebody who knew somebody and the whole place wept. And it wasn't just their own grief—they wept for other people's grief. When everyone's dancing and jumping up and down there's that deep well of pathos because everybody is connected."[64] The 930 million globally who watched U2 during the Super Bowl halftime show of February 3, 2002, saw a similar scroll, reacting with no doubt similar global grief. One author of a book about U2 fans thanked the band for "the Super Bowl appearance of 'Where the Streets Have No Name,' which provided me with an unexpected and emotional sense of closure to 9/11."[65]

George W. Bush's ascent to the White House coincided with an additional lobbying effort by Bono in dozens more trips across the Atlantic. Jubilee 2000 had morphed into "Drop the Debt," and so in January 2002, Bono joined his continuing interest in debt with two other policy issues— the AIDS epidemic and unfair trade agreements—into a new organization called DATA, for "Debt-AIDS-Trade-Africa," which he bankrolled along with Bill Gates and Ed Scott, another Silicon Valley tycoon.

One author identified DATA as the first time a celebrity had created his own think tank/lobbying firm and grassroots political interest group. DATA even hired two Washington lobbyists at nearly half a million dollars each for a year.[66] "Bono realized that he needed to play by the rules of Washington, and that's what we're doing," the organization explained.[67] To journalist James Traub, "DATA demonstrated that the singer was in this for the long haul, and that he cared not just about clarion calls but also about the tedious business of developing expertise and political organization."[68]

The "debt" in the new acronym shifted from targeting bilateral forgiveness from the United States, the United Kingdom, Italy, and France to multilateral institutions, such as the IMF and the World Bank. The added focus on trade came from a suggestion from Sheryl Sandberg, Larry Summers's chief of staff, to the effect that rewriting agreements could do more for Africa than debt reform.[69] In the mid-2000s, the rich countries that were ready to forgive $100 billion in bad loans were spending the same amount on agricultural subsidies that kept Africa, with 12 percent of the world's population, producing only 2 percent of world trade (down from 6 percent in 1980).[70] Trade was exhibit A in Bono's message of justice over charity. "Not letting the poorest of the poor put their products on our shelves whilst advertising the free market, that's a justice issue to me."[71]

Bono grasped the historical processes at work. "Two hundred years ago, it appears that very little difference existed in living standards between the Northern Hemisphere and the Southern Hemisphere. Today a very wide income gap exists. . . . The reason why Africa is still in the Middle Ages is largely to do with us, and our exploitation through French and British colonialism, but also in their present exploitation of unfair trade agreements, or old debts. . . . When you ask me to just accept that civilizations are just at a different level, there is a reason why they are."[72]

Bono's pitch on AIDS reflected his take on debt—that it was morally reprehensible to let "the biggest pandemic in the history of civilization" fester while solutions were obvious, available, and cheap. "It's bigger than the Black Death, which took a third of Europe in the Middle Ages. 6,500 Africans are dying every day of a preventable treatable disease."[73] In favor of generic AIDS cocktails, he fumed that "these drugs cost fucking nothing to make after research. At a time when people do not think that we are such a benign force in the world, we are letting people die for the stupidest of reasons: money! It is so fucked up!"[74]

In more restrained terms, he told President Bush that "you know 6,500 people dying every day of a preventable and treatable disease would not be acceptable anywhere else in the world other than Africa, and that before God and history this was a kind of racism that was unacceptable. And [Bush] agreed: 'Yeah, it's unacceptable. In fact, it's a kind of genocide.'"[75] In calling for a "Marshall Plan for Africa," Bono harkened back to a less selfish age when nations took on tremendous developmental challenges with great forethought.[76]

By December 2003, 20 million people worldwide had died of AIDS-related causes, and another 40 million lived with HIV/AIDS. Africa, with only 11 percent of the globe's population, harbored two-thirds of those with the disease. South Africa had the most cases of any country, afflicting about 20 percent of its adults—including Mandela's own son, who died of AIDS-related causes in 2005. To make matters worse, pharmaceutical corporations around the world either sued or put pressure on the South African government to ban cheaper generic antiretroviral drugs. As a result, South Africa's life expectancy and per capita gross national income were actually declining.[77] Sub-Saharan Africa's life expectancy would have been 63 rather than 47 years if not for HIV/AIDS.[78]

Fans were easily on board with DATA. At concerts, U2 asked fans to hold up their cell phones and sign up for the ONE campaign, a DATA initiative to fight global AIDS and extreme poverty. In the early 2000s, the Treasury Department received 20,000 e-mails from U2 fans about debt relief.

To the distaste of his bandmates—Larry marched against Bush's war in Iraq—and to a large extent his own, Bono had to lobby an administration whose policies he mostly abhorred.[79] But Bono turned out to be attractive to conservatives for several reasons.

First was his celebrity. Republicans accepted him with open arms since he seemed to give this most unpopular White House some hipness and some credibility with liberals. "He's charming, he's persuasive," explained pal Bob Geldof. "And the politicians can go home to their daughters and say: 'I had a meeting with Bono today.'"[80] National Security Advisor Condoleezza Rice admitted, "It's great to have a person who would not normally be identified with the president's development agenda as part of it."[81]

Second was Bono's willingness to revise his own beliefs. "I really have had to swallow my own prejudice at times. Because I was suspicious of the traditional Christian church, I tended to tar them all with the same brush. That was a mistake, because there are righteous people working in a whole rainbow of belief systems—from Hasidic Jews to right-wing Bible Belters to charismatic Catholics."[82]

Bono showed he could learn from conservatives just as they learned from him when, in the spring of 2002, he made a much-publicized trip to Africa with Bush's treasury secretary, Paul O'Neill. O'Neill at first refused to meet with Bono. "I thought he was just some pop star who wanted to use me." But during their meeting, O'Neill defied Bono: "If you want U.S. money to flow to Africa, take me to the green hills and show me what works." Bono smiled: "Let's set a date." "He's a serious person," O'Neill concluded. "He cares deeply about these issues, and you know what? He knows a lot about them."[83] The African trip covered Ghana, South Africa, Uganda, and Ethiopia in 11 days. The Republican remained skeptical of economic aid as the solution to development, but eventually he conceded that "in the right environment focused on growth, enterprise, and human development, aid works. Knowing it can work, we have a moral imperative to demand as much."[84]

At the same time, O'Neill convinced Bono of the necessity for freer trade in Africa, that "the future of Africa is in the hands of business and commerce," as Bono recalled. "And I knew that to be sort of true, but as much as I needed to, and it opened my mind to subjects like unfair trade relationships. It's a shock to discover that for all our talk of the free market, the poorest people on Earth are not allowed to put their products on our shelves in an evenhanded way. They have to negotiate all kinds of tariffs and taxes. It's not a level playing field."[85]

The third reason for Bono's good working relationship with conservatives was that he linked poverty in Africa to their all-consuming concern with the "global war on terror." After 9/11, Bono slyly worked the security angle and argued that "the roots of the present conflict are clearly the lack of conflict resolution in the area of the Middle East and the abject poverty of Africa." Poverty eradication would drain the pool of angry youth who might join militant organizations. He also avoided criticizing the U.S. war in Afghanistan.[86] To Bush in 2004, he again used the analogy of the Marshall Plan "to describe the strategic value of investing in Africa as a bulwark against future extremism, an argument your own Administration has made . . . the way the U.S. invested in Europe post-World War Two as a bulwark against Sovietism."[87]

Senator Rick Santorum, for one, was convinced and tried to persuade the White House that the Millennium Challenge Account, a massive aid program initiated by Bush, needed funding because it was "part of our war on terror."[88] Conservative television host Bill O'Reilly complimented Bono for "doing God's work"—an expression Bono himself had used with Bush months earlier. "We need people like you to command a worldwide audience and to get people at least thinking about this," O'Reilly continued. "I do agree that if America could take the lead it would turn public opinion around and help us in the war on terror."[89] In a larger sense, the Bush administration worried about Africa's "geo-strategic significance, with the U.S. seeking to foster military and security relationships which advance its own agenda."[90]

A fourth reason that Bono was appealing to conservatives is that he never threatened the capitalist system in word or deed. He may have preached some aid that swam against the tide of the free market, but only in a way that was already largely accepted by corporations. More commonly, he preached "trade not aid," or the dismantling of Western protectionist policies so as to improve Africa's chances in the global free market. "To understand commerce," he told *Rolling Stone* in 2014, "I think that's very important. If you told me 20 years ago that commerce took more people out of poverty than aid and development, I'd have scoffed." As one scholar explained, "Bono's hope in the promises of globalization is rooted in his belief that love can conquer all; this includes God, America, and capitalist markets."[91]

A fifth reason was, as one scholar has argued, that U2's messages have long been conservative in nature, even evangelical. The band long resisted the "dead end credo of 'sex, drugs, and rock and roll'" and rejected moral relativism. Instead, they sought to reaffirm eternal truths, such as beauty, goodness, individualism, temperance, justice, and love, and they argued for "an enduring moral order."[92] As Bono wrote to Bush, he flattered him but also reminded him of their shared conservative values: "Americans long to be reconnected to the original ideas that formed your great country, ideas that were out of fashion like duty, the sacred value of a life."[93]

The sixth reason and likely the most decisive of them all was Bono's own strong faith. Christians in the United States were not predisposed to fighting AIDS. Polls revealed that, in 2001, only 7 percent of U.S. evangelicals felt a responsibility to respond to AIDS and that more than half of U.S. Christians probably or definitely would not donate money to children orphaned by AIDS.[94]

To overcome such prejudice, Bono needed to connect. "The way to get to the right, as it happens, is through their religiosity." Again he harkened back to his Irish roots, this time to explain his ease with this constituency: "We have to find a way of working with the right on this—I knew that always. I mean it's just from growing up in the street by the way—in Dublin, North side of Dublin—you know, you find the tough guy, make him your friend—if you're my height."[95] He described U.S. evangelicals as "narrow-minded idealists," meaning that "if you can widen the aperture of that idealism, these people want to change the world. They want their lives to have meaning."[96]

Bono famously reduced to tears Senator Helms, the arch-conservative North Carolinian who once stated that AIDS was God's retribution against homosexuality, by telling Helms about the plight of children living with AIDS. Bono also used his deep knowledge of scriptures, recalling the biblical origins of Jubilee. "I was deeply impressed with him," said Helms. "He has depth that I didn't expect. He is led by the Lord to do something about the starving people in Africa." Likewise, Spencer Bachus, a Republican from Alabama, justified his support for debt relief on religious grounds: "Jubilee 2000 is a celebration of the 2000th birthday of Christ. . . . What more appropriate time to give to these poor in celebration of the birth of Jesus, who gave us life?"[97]

On June 13, 2001, at a Capitol Hill lunch, Helms promised Bono, "You'll never be an outsider. You'll always be a friend here." Bono returned the favor, saying the North Carolinian "did an incredible thing: he publicly repented for the way he had thought about HIV/AIDS. Politicians rarely do that. He really changed the way people on the right thought about this disease. People said to me: This is the devil himself you're going to meet, and his politics are just right of Attila the Hun. . . . But I found him to be a beautiful man with convictions that I wouldn't all agree with, but had to accept that he believed in them passionately."[98]

The Bush people suggested that Bono the Christian reach out to the faith community and specifically find Nashville-based country musicians who could help. In the summer of 2002, Bono made Jumbotron screen appearances at a dozen Christian music festivals. His three-minute speeches cited scriptures and enjoined the audience to love Africans as their neighbors.[99] He also met quietly with bands.

The response was overwhelming. Joe Foreman of Switchfoot admitted that the celebrity factor drew him: "I would not have dropped everything and booked a ticket at the last minute to hear a social worker discuss the problems in Africa. . . . I am a selfish, star-struck, rich, American, Anglo-Saxon fan of Bono." Third Day's Tai Anderson recalled that Bono "treated us with a lot of respect." Anderson took the stage repeatedly to ask fans to demand action from Bush. When Bush committed to massive funding against AIDS, recalled Anderson, "I got up and was running around the house: 'Democracy works! He does care!'" Those who put together Bono's announcements also produced two books, *The aWAKE Project* and *Mission: Africa*. Their nonprofit regularly mass e-mailed Christian musicians, informing them that "during the past year we've seen many of our most influential artists organize mission trips, conduct seminars on college campuses, include alerts in their CD liner notes, perform benefit concerts, and speak with conviction about the crisis both from stage and in interviews. And their fans are responding. In spades! Congressmen have been telling Bono's DATA team that they're hearing from constituents they NEVER hear from."[100]

In December 2002, Bono and other celebrities embarked on the "Heart of America" tour—seven states in seven days—to publicize DATA's causes to midwestern churches and other potentially conservative venues in the United States. In Lincoln, Nebraska; Louisville, Kentucky; and Greenfield, Iowa, as well as Chicago, Cincinnati, Indianapolis, and other settings, they visited truck stops and megachurches, and his team gave away 10,000 cards that could be sent to Congress or President Bush. Bono spoke the language of liberation theology and other progressive creeds, telling crowds about "God's preferential concern for the poor" and calling for "civil disobedience."

Yet he also invoked traditional Manichaean morality and righteous indignation: "There's a war going on between good and evil. And millions of children and millions of lives are being lost to greed, to bureaucracy, and to a church that's been asleep. And it sends me out of my mind with anger."[101] And, as any good politician, he flattered his audiences: "We're here largely because politicians have told us people in the Midwest don't care about issues outside of the US. We believe there's kind of a moral compass that lives here."[102]

Pastor Bill Hybels of Willow Creek, a megachurch in suburban Chicago, met with the singer, and "I came away convinced that Bono's faith is genuine, his vision to relieve the tragic suffering in Africa is God-honoring, and his prophetic challenge to the U.S. church must be taken seriously."[103]

There were some skeptics among U.S. Christians. *Christianity Today*, for example, doubted that Bono's version of Christianity outside organized religion was feasible or desirable. "A Christian's pleading for social justice without worshiping God regularly within the community of the church is little more than activism for its own sake." The leading Christian publication did not get "a sense that he felt much respect for the evangelical culture he was lecturing" and in turn lectured Bono on the fact that "Christians were bringing relief to suffering Africans in the same decade that U2 poured millions into its bloated Zoo TV and PopMart tours."[104]

Figure 4.3. Bono at the 2005 G8 Summit in Scotland, where world leaders made massive financial commitments to the Make Poverty History campaign. Left to right: Prime Minister Tony Blair, singer/activist Bob Geldof, Kenyan Nobel Prize–winner Wangari Maathai, and writer Richard Curtis at a press conference. *Bruce Adams/Daily Mail/REX USA*

But many more seemed to respond to Bono's message. Dan Haseltine from the band Jars of Clay stated that "U2 has been a model of sorts. They have been a good example of people living lives in the reality of the Gospel. Lives that spend more time doing than explaining." Jars of Clay followed the example, setting up missions to find clean water and clean blood for Africans struggling with HIV and AIDS. Michael W. Smith wrote the song "We Can't Wait Any Longer," "inspired by the work with Bono and DATA." In 2004, several Christian bands issued a collection of U2 covers called *In the Name of Love: Artists United for Africa*, a fund-raiser for AIDS charities.[105] By 2003, Bono was praising U.S. churches for leading the struggle against AIDS.[106]

By mid-decade, Episcopalian congregations were celebrating "U2charists," using the band's music during communion services to talk about global reconciliation, social justice, and caring for one's neighbors. "Perhaps U2 doesn't look (or sound) like most Christian musicians," wrote one Christian author. "But what could be more Christlike than what they do and what they produce?"[107] Another posited that "U2 might be thought of as a sort of ecclesia."[108] Many others shared T. Bone Burnett's observation that, with its spiritual cleansing and communal spirit, "a U2 concert is what a church should be."[109]

Bono's lobbying with the Vatican and U.S. churches and missionaries also helped move politicians. Bono had long adopted the preaching style of nineteenth-century revivalists, couching his homilies to U.S. politicians as moving forward human agency rather than waiting on divine providence.[110] Two preachers recall meeting Bono on Capitol Hill in 2002 along with "25 or so" representatives of lending institutions, charities, and academic and religious organizations. To them, the singer explained "why his interest in Africa was something other than passing fad, a celebrity cause—why in fact it grew out of his deepest commitments about the way the world is and ought to be, out of his love for and loyalty to Jesus and the gospel of the kingdom." The preachers were convinced that Bono was the "kind of person" who had achieved "a graceful seamlessness between liturgy and learning and life."[111]

Congressman Sonny Callahan of Alabama hesitated to support debt relief because it "would encourage the World Bank and others to continue to make bad loans and leave poor countries to have to borrow and get into debt all over again."[112] Yet he changed his mind when, according to Callahan, "I incurred the wrath of the church community worldwide."[113] "There were priests in the pulpit. Priests and pastors sermonizing on debt relief on Sundays, telling their congregations to tell Callahan to take care of this, including my own bishop. Eventually I gave in. What else could I have done?" When the debt relief bill encountered resistance that brought it to a congressional "floor fight," the Reverend Billy Graham agreed to make a two-minute video in support of Jubilee that was sent to Congress's holdouts.[114]

In 2003, the Bush administration responded to this alliance of liberals and conservatives to pledge $15 billion in five years to fight HIV/AIDS. The President's Emergency Plan for AIDS Relief (PEPFAR) made available antiretroviral drugs for 900,000 people as well as 11 million bed nets.[115] In 2004, after much more lobbying from Bono and conservative politicians, PEPFAR received $2.4 billion, and DATA called it the largest increase in U.S. assistance to poor countries in 40 years.

Jeffrey Sachs praised the U2 singer: "Once again, Bono played a unique role in pulling the coalition together, not just as a celebrity and entertainer, but as a rare individual who could reach deeply into the hearts and minds of a remarkable range of individuals."[116] Bono and DATA were also instrumental in lobbying the Senate to pass an extension of President Clinton's African Growth and Opportunity Act until 2015. The *Washington Post* editorialized that the coalition that united Bono with the business lobby and the Congressional Black Caucus "made the impossible possible."[117]

In mid-2005, Bono revived his role as chief spokesperson for antipoverty groups. Bono's discursive goal for the Make Poverty History (MPH) campaign was to change the terms of debate about aid to Africa from considering it a charity case to a question of justice. Its policy goal was to pressure the 2005 G8 Summit to commit to reducing African poverty.

The MPH's flagship events were the Live8 concerts, which, like Live Aid 20 years earlier, brought artists together from around the world. Unlike Live Aid, Live8 and MPH intended to raise only awareness, not funds, but it still produced $12 million for relief projects in Africa from sponsors, merchandising, and television and DVD rights.[118] The hundred or so participating artists performed in 11 cities around the world, and the multimedia broadcast of the concert in Hyde Park, London, reached an audience of 3 billion.[119] Additional millions watched the made-for-television movie *The Girl in the Café* on BBC and HBO and in South Africa. The film's writer and producer was Richard Curtis, who campaigned for MPH.[120]

The commitments made by the finance ministers at the June 2005 summit were mind-boggling: $40 billion for debt relief for the poorest 18 countries, with the World Bank, the IMF, and the African Development Bank taking hits; a potential expansion of the program to 27 countries and $55 billion in 18 months; and an extra $25 billion in aid to Africa in 2010, including universal access to HIV drugs.[121]

On hearing of these pledges, Bono said, "I would not say this is the end of extreme poverty, but it is the beginning of the end."[122]

Many again cited the work of Bono and his colleagues in securing these pledges. French President Jacques Chirac admitted that the campaign for debt relief "undoubtedly had an influence on the decisions taken during the G8 Summit in Gleneagles."[123] "It's difficult to imagine much of it would have been done without [Bono]," confirmed Canadian Prime

Minister Paul Martin.[124] "I remember vividly watching Bono work the back halls at the G8 Summit in Gleneagles, Scotland, and I was really struck by how up to speed he was," said a former development official. "Geldof was there too and, though he worked hard, he was not in the same league as Bono." "It's easy to snipe," said another, "but I don't think there is a single public official who has done more to raise awareness of Africa or to mobilize action than Bono. If he ended up winning the Nobel Peace Prize it would not be such a great stretch."[125]

* * *

In fact, in the first half decade of the twenty-first century, Bono's name was floated as possible president of the World Bank, and in 2003 and again in 2005, he was nominated for the Nobel Peace Prize. Bono was so successful in melding the worlds of charity and entertainment that *Time* magazine proclaimed 2005 the "year of charitainment."[126]

The lack of cynicism meeting Bono's activism was partly a reflection of the seriousness in world affairs following the attacks of 9/11 and its disenchantment with irony. People needed to believe that, in the face of global terror, at least some of the world's problems could be alleviated, perhaps even solved. And suddenly, poverty and disease seemed solvable for the few tens of billions of dollars requested compared to hundreds of billions sunk each year into wars in Iraq and Afghanistan.

Singer Chris Martin of Coldplay said of U2, "It's amazing that the biggest band in the world has so much integrity and passion in their music. Our society is thoroughly screwed, fame is a ridiculous waste of time and celebrity culture is disgusting. There are only a few people around brave enough to talk out against it, who use their fame in a good way."[127] Few disagreed—for now.

5

CONSOLIDATION AND CRITICISM, 2006–2015

I'm not stupid. I'm aware of the futility of rock 'n' roll music, but I'm also aware of its power.—Bono[1]

U2 went into relative decline after 2005—again. Their resurgence as the grown-up, heartfelt soul of popular music that began in 2000 was coming to an end. To be sure, U2 was more popular and richer than ever. In 2005, *Billboard* magazine declared U2 its top "money maker," totaling its album, digital, and box-office sales at over $255 million.[2] Their 2009–2011 world tour was the highest grossing in history, raking in over $736 million, in addition to having the highest average gross per concert and highest average attendance.[3]

But U2's creative juices seemed to be drying up. Lyrics and melodies on *How to Dismantle an Atomic Bomb* (2005), *No Line on the Horizon* (2009), and *Songs of Innocence* (2014) were less inspired than on their seminal albums. While still admirably experimenting with music, Bono and the boys, in their early fifties, seemed to be entering the final stage of their career. The "outer space" theme of their 360 Tour seemed to telegraph that they did not know in which direction to go artistically. Bono and The Edge were also embroiled in the troubled Broadway production of *Spider-Man: Turn Off the Dark*, for which they wrote the music and lyrics.[4]

After the great victories of the first half of the 2000s, U2's activism also suffered an almost inevitable lessening, albeit a relative one. Bono's unprecedented breakthroughs earlier in the decade could hardly be topped. Critics also assailed the band and especially Bono on their activism. There was some well-considered skepticism about how aid from the West could really help Africa and even accusations that it could make things worse. Other criticisms revealed envy, naïveté, or just deep cynicism, the very instincts that U2 had always fought against.

Backed by the band, Bono sympathized with some doubts and fought back against others. He learned from critics to adjust his expectations without modifying his basic message or strategy. He also described the early twenty-first century as "a time of great geopolitical unrest. The majority of people in the world no longer idolize Western ideals of justice, freedom, and equality."[5] More important, he consolidated his activism into a long-term lobbying organization and in doing so solidified his reputation as the leading activist of the early twenty-first century. He was reportedly nominated again for the Nobel Peace Prize in 2006, 2010, and 2013, bringing his nominations to five. In 2008, he was awarded the Nobel Man of Peace prize among many other humanitarian awards he received in the 2000s.[6]

* * *

As in every decade since the 1980s, the U2 community was involved in human rights work, but this time it was also able to celebrate a few milestones.

Ali continued her work, begun in the mid-1990s, with the Chernobyl Children's Project (CCP). After her first visit to the still-dangerous radiation site in 1993, she returned seven times in 10 years, driving what Bono described as "convoys of supplies from Ireland to Russia," at times bringing orphaned children back to Ireland.[7] The CCP was the subject of a 2004 Oscar-winning documentary, *Chernobyl Heart*.

The Edge's most prominent humanitarian work was his cofounding of Music Rising, which got donations from 1,500 musicians and put instruments back in the hands of over 3,000 U.S. central gulf musicians devastated by Hurricane Katrina in 2005. It also reopened Preservation Hall in New Orleans and helped rebuild the music programs of churches and schools affected by the hurricane. It then moved on to help other musicians and areas of the United States impacted by natural disasters. In 2014, Music Rising supported Tulane University's launch of a program of lectures, symposia, and accredited learning modules for children from kindergarten to high school. [8]

The band, meanwhile, participated in several events to help Haiti after the January 2010 earthquake near Port-au-Prince that killed hundreds of thousands and reduced much of the capital to rubble. Within days of the disaster, Bono and The Edge teamed up with hip-hop artists Jay-Z and Rihanna to produce the song "Stranded (Haiti Mon Amour)." They performed it for the "Hope for Haiti Now" telethon and album. On the fourth anniversary of the tragedy, U2 offered a miniconcert at the Help Haiti Home benefit. [9]

In late 2010, U2 rejoiced at the freedom to travel that the human rights crusader Aung San Suu Kyi won from the Burmese government. The band had a long history with her. When they were given the Freedom of Dublin award in 2000, she was also honored in her absence. The Edge realized that he knew nothing about her, but soon he and Bono found her story deeply compelling. An academic at Oxford University, Aung San Suu Kyi left her British husband and family to return to Burma to lead the National League for Democracy. She won democratic elections in 1990, but the brutal military junta kept her under house arrest. On 2000's *All That You Can't Leave Behind*, U2 celebrated her sacrifice on "Walk On." The Burmese government banned the album, threatening a 20-year sentence against anyone who bought it. Starting in 2000, U2 urged fans to pressure Britain to boycott meetings with Southeast Asian ministers to protest Burma's many political prisoners. [10]

In Dublin in June 2012, Bono awarded Aung San Suu Kyi Amnesty International's Ambassador of Conscience Award, which she earned in 2009 but could not collect from prison (she also won the Nobel Peace Prize in 1991). "There is no one on this island who doesn't understand how costly the word freedom is. How difficult the word justice is to live by. How quixotic peace can be," he said, once again using his Irishness to connect to global activists. [11]

U2 also saluted the passing of Nelson Mandela, who died on December 5, 2013. The South African leader, along with Archbishop Desmond Tutu, were formative influences on the band as they cut their teeth on human rights issues in the 1980s. When Mandela died, Bono credited his "anti-apartheid and anti-poverty" message for teaching him that "poverty is not a natural condition." [12] A few days before the South African's death, The Edge, humbled that U2 had been asked to write "Ordinary

Love" for the biopic "Mandela," explained that "we've been working for Madiba [Mandela's clan name] since we were teenagers. And so it's kind of coming full circle now."[13] Bono and Ali's last day on the job was paying their respects at the funeral along with other global dignitaries (see figure 5.1).

Even with Bono incapacitated, the band carried on with its activism. On December 1, 2014, after their singer injured himself in a bike accident in New York's Central Park, "U2 Minus 1" went through with a surprise concert in Times Square, enlisting Coldplay's Chris Martin and Bruce Springsteen each to sing two songs to mark World AIDS Day. Bill Clinton introduced the band, and Barack Obama sent a video message. After decades of activism, Bono noted from Dublin that "the world reached a tipping point in the fight against AIDS—more people were newly added to life-saving treatment than were newly infected with the virus. . . . Today, 13 million people have access to life-saving treatment, up from 300,000 just over ten years ago."[14]

Figure 5.1. Bono and wife Ali Hewson with U.S. President Barack Obama and First Lady Michelle Obama as they get ready to leave the Nelson Mandela memorial service in December 2013. *Official White House photo by Pete Souza*

After the mid-2000s, Bono also continued his humanitarian and lobbying work, mostly through the ONE Campaign. It was founded in May 2004 by 11 organizations and officially merged with DATA in 2008. "Campaign" was a misnomer since ONE was not dedicated to a short-term goal but rather a full-blown, permanent advocacy organization whose leadership included establishment figures from politics and philanthropy and whose staff lobbied legislatures, raised funds, and produced policy briefs. By 2007, the network had received $22 million from the Bill and Melinda Gates Foundation, and both the Republican and the Democratic National Committees had endorsed its campaign against child hunger in Africa.[15]

In 2007, Bono said that ONE "is becoming like the National Rifle Association in its firepower, but acts in the interests of the world's poor."[16] The statement was telling.

In the evolution of U2's activism, ONE marked a seminal moment. For the first time, a permanent organization existed to institutionalize and therefore carry on the work of Bono, who in the late 1990s had piggy-backed onto the Jubilee 2000 campaign as little more than a spokesperson. Now his good works were the full-time occupation of a permanent staff and devoted leaders. In theory, they would be able to continue long after the singer left the organization.

ONE embraced all of DATA's causes—debt, AIDS, trade, and Africa—and added a concern for making more transparent the activities of mining, oil, and gas corporations. Its strategy was to help pass laws that pressured these corporations to disclose all payments they made to governments. "One of the biggest obstacles is corruption," said Bono. "There is a cure for that—a vaccine. We call it transparency . . . it's really a revolution. A transparency revolution." He championed the Lugar-Carding amendment of the Dodd-Frank bill passed by the U.S. Congress because "now energy companies traded on American exchanges will have to reveal every payment they make to government officials."[17]

As always, ONE used Bono to drum up media attention. The name originated in the desire for Western governments to devote 1 percent of their budgets to foreign aid (they gave about a third of that), but it was also logical to take the organization's name from one of U2's most beloved songs, ironically one about a lovers' breakup but whose lyrics were reinterpreted to invoke not only romance but also unity among peoples.[18] During the performance of the song on U2's 2005 tour, Bono usually took breaks from singing—notably, a 14-minute break during a Washington, D.C., show, as Larry informed him grumpily—to discuss projects "to make poverty history" and ask concertgoers to sign up with their cell phones. "People want to be a part of that," Bono said, "and they feel they are a part of that, part of the generation that can actually turn the super-tanker of indifference around."[19] Bono also transformed the vague lyrics of "Where the Streets Have No Name" to describe "this notion, the jour-ney of equality . . . a journey to that other place. . . . That lyric was written in a dusty field in northern Ethiopia. And I can finally make sense of it."[20]

With the help of Bob Geldof, Bono pressed his ONE case to U.S. and European audiences by guest-editing special issues of *The Independent* (United Kingdom), *Vanity Fair* (United States), *Libération* (France), *Asa-shi Shimbum* (Japan), *Bild* (Germany), *La Stampa* (Italy), and *The Globe and Mail* (Canada) in addition to BBC Radio 4's *Today* show. Bono regularly penned op-eds and open letters in the world's leading news-papers and appealed to tens of millions on television, attracting tens of thousands of new members for ONE.[21]

ONE perpetuated Bono's successful lobbying. In July 2005, after mil-lions had joined the campaign, the organization urged members to contact their U.S. senators to support a $100 million AIDS and malaria amend-ment. Twenty-five thousand calls poured in, and the amendment passed.[22]

By 2015, ONE had over 6 million global members. It claimed to have helped increase the number of Africans under AIDS medication from 50,000 in 2002 to 9 million and "helping secure $95 billion in debt relief for poor countries over the past decade." In 2013, Bono noted that the percentage of those living in extreme poverty on the planet had fallen from 43 percent in 1990 to 21 percent in 2010. If this trend continued, he predicted, extreme poverty would be eliminated by 2030. More broadly, Bono told interviewer Charlie Rose in 2013, voided African debts had put 51 million children into school in the previous 10 years. He also praised evangelicals and the White House for saving 9 million AIDS victims. The Global Fund to Fight AIDS, Tuberculosis and Malaria, known simply as "the Global Fund" and to which ONE contributed, "saves a staggering 4,000 lives a day," he added.[23]

"I love these numbers," said Bono. "These are sexy numbers. They rhyme somewhere in my head."[24]

Bono also helped found two somewhat less sexy and more controversial projects. Product (RED), formed in January 2006 with Bobby Shriver, was an effort to involve large corporations to induce consumers to make a habit of charitable giving. The idea was not simply to have corporations donate part of their profits to (RED) but to make specific (RED)-branded products that consumers would choose to buy precisely because they contributed to ONE-type programs. The incentive for corporations is that they would increase sales based on the desire for consumers to direct their purchasing power toward these products. American Express marketed a (RED) credit card, Converse developed (RED) sneakers, and the Gap put out its (RED) T-shirt. Many of these projects were made out of African materials and/or produced in Africa.[25] Joining the fray were Apple, Emporio Armani, Hallmark, Starbucks, and Motorola. Apple notably raised $76 million for (RED). Specifically, (RED) raised funds for the Global Fund. In 2010, the Home Box Office network aired a (RED)-produced documentary, *The Lazarus Effect*, that highlighted how millions of Africans on antiretroviral medication, like the biblical Lazarus, had "come back to life."[26]

The initiative was part of a growing trend in corporate social responsibility (CSR). CSR began in the 1980s and 1990s when philanthropy became part and parcel of corporate strategic plans. Product (RED) was a type of CSR called "cause-related marketing," in which consumers would be told that a portion of the proceeds of specific purchases would go not to an organization but rather to a specific cause, such as HIV/AIDS.[27]

In 2012, ONE acquired (RED) as one of its divisions. As such, (RED) pursued its own initiatives, such as a partnership that kicked off during the Super Bowl on February 2, 2014. One commercial had U2 performing a new song, "Invisible," and generating $10 million for the Global Fund through a new (RED) sponsor, Bank of America. The bank would also raise awareness of mother-to-child transmission of AIDS among its tens of millions of customers, with the goal of ending that form of transmission by 2015. Early in that year, (RED) declared that it had raised over $300 million for the Global Fund and fighting AIDS in eight African countries.[28]

Stemming from the same impulse to create more—and more just—trade for Africa, in 2005 Ali and Bono created a second project called Edun—"nude" spelled backwards. Edun was a high-end for-profit fair-trade fashion line intended to be produced in Africa. The idea was to

improve the skills of workers and make Africa a greater player in globalization and avoid the stigma of helplessness. "Africa needs more globalization than less," explained Bono. Ali added that Africans said "thank
God" when they heard Edun was for-profit; they wanted it to be sustainable.[29]

Reflecting Bono's own growing pragmatism since the 1980s, Ali reflected that "times have changed and people realise that they are not
going to be able to change the world they live in by burning an effigy at
the palace gates. The revolution is happening in your house, in your
purse, in your wallet, in how you spend your money. Shopping is politics."

Her own attachment to the continent began in childhood. "I was eight
or nine when we got a television, and the images were of African famine.
At that age it makes a huge impression on you. Then when Live Aid
happened it was hard to believe that Africa hadn't moved on." When she
and her husband followed Live Aid with a trip to Ethiopia, she was
"shocked by the number of Irish people there. . . . It seems to be that
everywhere there is a disaster, Irish people come out of the woodwork
and they are there trying to fix things."[30]

However well intentioned, Edun was less than successful. The couple
invested millions of their own in the venture, but it ran up against supply
chain and quality control problems and lost more than $38 million by
2011, even after the couple sold a 49 percent stake to Louis Vuitton Moët
Hennessey in 2009. It survived partly by moving some production to Peru
and China. Yet, according to Edun, 85 percent of its spring 2014 collection was produced in sub-Saharan Africa (see figure 5.2).[31]

As the 2000s turned into the 2010s, Bono was the recipient of much
criticism for his activism and his socially conscious business ventures. He
brushed off most of it, but some of it clearly transformed his thinking,
while some of it did not but perhaps should have.

First, there were several objections to the very notion of celebrity
activism. One was that celebrities' interests tended to be superficial and
fleeting. Attention tended to focus on the star, not the cause, and "the
spectacle culture of celebrity activists makes it impossible to provide in-
depth and extensive information." And once a star's attention flittered
away from a cause, so would donors.[32] Audiences that followed celebrities also tended to be least engaged in politics and therefore ineffective

Figure 5.2. **Ali Hewson with husband Bono promoting the ONE Campaign and the (RED) clothing line in a textile factory in Butha Buthe, Lesotho, May 17, 2006.** *Kim Haughton/REX USA*

in applying the kind of sophisticated, protracted pressure necessary to bring about change.[33]

Even if stars were steadfast and successful at raising funds, shoveling massive amounts to one cause might lead to the neglect of other, "less media-friendly" causes. Or celebrities, seeking the spotlight, might focus more on crises such as natural disasters rather than ongoing structural problems. An earthquake is more attention grabbing than trade liberalization. Similarly, celebrities drained attention away from serious experts with detailed knowledge.[34]

Meanwhile, many were skeptical that celebrities endorsed charities in order to generate free publicity for themselves as humanitarians. After all, U2's Live Aid performance in 1985 also turned out to be one of the band's greatest marketing moments. One scholar dismissed Live8 20 years later because it "once again provided a venue for the free advertising of celebrities," not to mention of corporations, such as Motorola. The big acts also crowded out smaller, local artists and overshadowed one of the largest public protests in the history of Scotland. [35]

A close corollary was that celebrities, despite their image as philanthropists, actually contributed relatively small donations to the world of philanthropy. In 2013, a typical year, not a single celebrity made *The Chronicle of Philanthropy's* list of 50 most generous donors. [36] The Irish press paid particular attention to U2's finances and estimated Bono's net worth at half a billion dollars. Bono responded that U2 kept a low profile with its donations. They spent €5 million for Music Generation, a music education program in Ireland, as well as an additional €12 million for African causes, and journalist Niall Stokes defended them, writing, "The fact is that the band do stuff all the time below the radar." Otherwise, it was true that U2 and Bono mostly raised money from others. They were primarily activists and lobbyists, not philanthropists. [37]

Celebrities, too, tended to raise the costs of activism and thus get corporations involved, which could distort the goals of activists. The Red Cross had a "director of celebrity outreach," and some celebrities, such as Angelina Jolie, retained firms, such as the Global Philanthropy Group, to recruit staff, bring in experts, and help activists figure out goals. [38] Others faulted celebrities for *not* gaining access and instead losing their influence when they tried to change the system from the inside, as Bono did. "In fact, having access can sometimes reduce your influence," said Kumi Naidoo, an activist who worked alongside Bono in 2005. "You think that because a powerful government official says roughly what you want to hear, you have made progress, but then at the first opportunity they make a U-turn or lower the bar." [39]

Stepping back even further, scholar Dan Brockington saw celebrity advocacy as another manifestation of "elite rule" in a "post-democracy," which he defined as "politics that are characterised by a loss of democratic verve and the corresponding rise of government by elite, and particularly corporate elites." He explained that celebrities actually engaged the public much less than assumed yet that elites believed that celebrities somehow embodied "the affective will of the people." "Celebrity advocacy is by and for the elites," he concluded. [40]

Bono had a realistic view of the limits and pitfalls of celebrity activism. "A lot of our work in the '80s was very naïve," he admitted, without regretting any of it. When asked if some politicians might agree in public to go along with his demands only to associate themselves with his fame, he said, "I can't worry too much about that. In Guyana people have a life expectancy of 47 years. And they're spending as much on repaying their loans to the West as they are on educating their people. So I don't think I can be too worried about who I'm sitting down with." When asked if politicians used him, Bono replied, "I'm available to be used, that is the deal here. I'll step out with anyone, but I'm not a cheap date." And Bono refused to bankroll schemes such as DATA personally, he said, to prevent the accusation of vanity.[41]

Otherwise, in an editorial titled "I Am a Witness. What Can I Do?," Bono wrote that he expected to be attacked as a rock star who preached to others but also that he witnessed too much suffering and bravery with his own eyes to leave him any choice. He defended celebrities who had "made a dent on the pop consciousness with Live Aid and 8, Red Nose Day, Comic Relief and Make Poverty History."[42]

A second set of criticisms posited that aid from the West, from celebrities or anyone else, robbed Africans of their agency and therefore worsened their lot. "Bono can't help Africans by stealing their voice," wrote George Monbiot in *The Guardian* in 2013, stating one of the most persistent criticisms—that westerners who advocated for "aid" to poor areas were in fact extending underdevelopment by reinforcing stereotypes. Images of a "dark," scary, helpless Africa could be perpetuated, and one scholar wrote that, given such representations, "Africa emerges as an unworldly continent void of intelligence, will or capacity to take care of itself" and that the West, in contrast, appears to be disinterested in its desire to help Africa. Such images "end up repeating and maintaining western authority over Africa."[43]

Critics, for instance, pounced on Bono's participation in Band Aid 30 in 2014, when he joined other European pop stars to re-record "Do They Know It's Christmas?" 30 years after the original. Bono was the only performer to return from the previous recording. This time the single benefited victims of Ebola in Africa, and it quickly became the fastest-selling single of the year. Bono's line was "Well tonight, we're reaching out and touching you," perhaps intended to dampen fears of touching anyone connected to Ebola. But British-Ghanaian rapper Fuse ODG pulled out of the recording after seeing the song's lyrics, which included describing Africa as a place "where a kiss of love can kill you and there's death in every tear" and "There is no peace and joy in West Africa this Christmas."

"Beyond the offensive lyrics," wrote the rapper, "I, like many others, am sick of the whole concept of Africa—a resource-rich continent with unbridled potential—always being seen as diseased, infested and poverty-stricken. In fact, seven out of 10 of the world's fastest growing economies are in Africa." "It's worth doing it for the money and the money is needed," agreed another critic. "However, it comes at a cost and the cost is the way in which Africa is being portrayed to the rest of the world" by possibly spreading fear and hurting tourism and trade on the continent.[44] "What is missing, invisible, off the agenda" in such representations of Africa, wrote Harry Browne, "is any belief that economic development can be a mode of collective self-determination, opening up a realm of freedom for the poor beyond that envisioned for them by billionaires."[45]

A corollary was that Western charity was essentially for the West, not Africa. "The trope of celebrity humanitarian," explained Browne, "functions as a redemption fantasy, . . . wherein inhabitants of the Global South are discursively positioned as the backdrop against which 'global good guys' can enhance their sense of themselves, and the reputation of the nation they represent, with insufficient attention to their own participation in relations of domination."[46] Damon Albarn, the singer of Blur, similarly advanced that "Bono is very well-meaning and has probably got a very good heart, but the idea of them and a thousand people, all tanked, all toasting this kind of great sentiment—the level of hypocrisy in all standing up for Third World debt to be abolished—it's profoundly Western."[47]

Browne packed these and other criticisms in his 2013 *The Frontman*, arguing that Bono had spent his career "amplifying elite discourses, advocating ineffective solutions, patronizing the poor, and kissing the arses of the rich and powerful." The singer also allegedly saw "the developed, especially Africa [with a] mix of traditional missionary and commercial colonialism, in which the poor world exists as a task for the rich world to complete."[48]

One report found that the Live8 concerts of 2005 did not change the already negative perceptions that viewers had about Africa and even worsened them for some. Charity organizations such as World Development Movement, Christian Aid, and Action Aid denounced the lack of African voices and paucity of black artists at the concerts. Donald Steinberg of the International Crisis Group noted that "there is a tendency for celebrities to treat Africa as a victim on a Jerry Lewis telethon. For many of us who believe that the future of Africa lies in real democratic governance, in trade and investment, in empowering the middle class, this conveys a message that's actually counterproductive."[49]

Bono responded to criticisms of Live8 by admitting that "personally, yes I think it was a mistake to not have more African artists." However, he pointed out that Youssou N'Dour and many other Africans performed in Johannesburg that day and that it was the media that chose to ignore the venue.[50]

Product (RED) and even DATA also came in for criticism from the many who doubted the intentions of the corporate world, making up a third and sometimes quite serious set of criticisms. Three scholars, for example, found that the level of secrecy of (RED) was suspect: "Not enough is known about the actual impact of CSR activities in developing countries." They did find that in 2006, Armani sold 44,000 (RED) sunglasses, 2,700 (RED) watches, and 70,000 (RED) clothing items and leather accessories and that 8 percent of its retail sales value went to the Global Fund. But they argued that "the benefits of RED's cause-related marketing are located most heavily in building brand image and less in the actual boosting of sales of individual RED products."

A related criticism was that such CSR made corporations look like saviors, while governments in reality did most of the heavy lifting of development. As of early 2008, for example, the Global Fund had gathered public contributions of $9.2 billion, while private donations amounted to only $460 million. They also noted that while (RED) purchased its goods from African factories, it made "no explicit attempt . . . to implement better working, social or environmental conditions on production." "Bono cannot be so naïve to think that the conditions in the factories he tours remain the same when he isn't there," added the director of the National Labor Committee for Worker and Human Rights.[51]

Skepticism about business was intertwined with wariness about celebrities and the lack of African agency. One scholar complained of charity concerts' "free advertising" for artists, cities, record companies, instrument manufacturers, and sponsors and added that Africans themselves were invisible, thus giving the lie to claims of "oneness." Africa thus became "an empty signifier, waiting to be provided both meaning and purpose," and Bono "continues to view Africa as an exploitable resource, as an unlimited labor force and potential market. . . . Africa is positioned in business terms."[52] Two other scholars argued that "the complex scripts of race, gender, and global economic inequality are ignored with justifications that 'AIDS is an emergency,'" while consumption and trade relations remained unaddressed. (RED) also "provides an easy solution to current crises in international development—one that enables corporations to raise their CSR profile without substantially changing their normal business practices while consumers engage in low-cost heroism without meaningfully increasing their awareness of global production-consumption relations or the struggles of living with HIV/AIDS."[53]

Browne gave the example that "DATA chose to work in cooperation with First World pharmaceutical companies, paying the full prices for their products, rather than directly challenging their medical patents." And in 2013, *The Guardian* upbraided the ONE campaign for praising the New Alliance for Food Security and Nutrition, which, it said, would "allow foreign companies to grab [African countries'] land, patent their seeds and monopolise their food markets." It noted that ONE's board was "largely composed of multimillionaires, corporate aristocrats and US enforcers," such as former U.S. secretary of state Condoleezza Rice. The Gates Foundation was notably close to food giant Monsanto and other corporations that allegedly aimed to solve poverty by producing more food or otherwise gaining "measurable results." Poverty, critics said, came not from insufficient food but from "problems with equality, with access, with education"—markers less easily measurable than food production. Historian Nick Cullather saw Bono, Gates, and Sachs as "a parvenu faction in international philanthropy" aiming to reclaim the mid-century Green Revolution's "development-without-industry agenda."[54]

Bono responded that issues such as the exploitation of African labor "are very serious but six and a half thousand Africans dying [of AIDS per week] is more serious." To the left, whose suspicion of big business he found "wholly unjustified," he said, "I don't see this as selling out. I see this as ganging up on the problem." More broadly, he defended Product (RED) as a response to the reality of runaway consumerism: people spend their money on frivolous goods rather than donate to charity, so those goods might as well include donations. (RED) "was an attempt to piggyback on the great companies," he explained, "to create heat and excitement around the issue of solving a problem." He also admitted his dependence on the superrich: "I couldn't do anything that I do without the Gates Foundation." To those who accused (RED) of encouraging simply more consumerism, its president, Tansin Smith, responded, "We're not encouraging people to buy more, but if they're going to buy a pair of Armani sunglasses, we're trying to get a cut of that for a good cause." Gates himself justified (RED) by explaining that "the companies involved in the (RED) campaign draw in new customers who want to be associated with a good cause. That might be the tipping point that leads people to pick one product over another." "Another crucial benefit . . . to businesses that do good work" was that "they will find it easier to recruit and retain great employees." By 2013, Bono had adopted Gates's term "creative capitalism," arguing that it "has probably pulled more people out of poverty than any other ideology." He even called (RED)-associated companies "heroic (and—shock, horror—we want them to make money for their shareholders because that will make [Red] sustainable)." As one scholar concluded of Bono's rationalizations, he "has made his peace with commoditization if it will save lives."[55]

Perhaps more important, Bono failed to respond to several criticisms expressed by scholars and journalists, if he was even aware of them. It seems that he was more mindful of the fourth set of criticisms, to the effect that money was not the solution to underdevelopment; eliminating corruption and incompetence was.[56]

In her 2009 book *Dead Aid: Why Aid Is Not Working and How There Is a Better Way for Africa*, development expert Dambisa Moyo argued that aid to Africa was counterproductive. Since 1970, the continent received $300 billion in aid, yet it continued to be poor and its governments corrupt. "Not only is aid easy to steal, as it is usually provided directly to African governments, but it also makes control over government worth fighting for. And, perhaps most importantly, the influx of aid can undermine domestic saving and investment," wrote scholar Niall Ferguson. Moyo herself derided the type of assistance championed by Bono as "glamour aid." Others pointed out that the millions supposedly raised by Live Aid in 1985 were never systematically accounted for, and Ethiopia remained poor. The *Times* of London added that debt forgiveness would "let Africa's kleptomaniac leaders 'off the hook'" and called for internal reform before any red could be wiped off Africa's ledger. One of the fiercest critics of Western aid, William Easterly, highlighted not only the paternalism and lack of accountability of aid "planners" but also the lack of incentives for those on the ground who, for example, distributed bed nets to prevent malaria.[57]

Aid and debt forgiveness also stifled state-led industrialization and development, wrote Cullather, because they required "structural adjustments including dismantling national food schemes and systems of credit, import quotas, price controls, and reserve stocks. . . . National governments pushed farmers to shift prime irrigated lands to production for export." Such changes opened up economies to globalization but also increased food insecurity.[58]

A final criticism of aid, specifically of debt forgiveness, was that it meant little concretely. Only half of official development aid actually reached the poor. Much of it was not funds or equipment but technical assistance or expert advice, which did not come cheap. The most expensive "aid" often went to security, for example, in the Middle East. Much of "debt forgiveness," meanwhile, was for a debt that was not being repaid anyway, including interest. "Forgiving it," wrote Homi Kharas, "has done little to increase the amounts available for real development problems like schooling, clinics, and infrastructure in the short term. Its real value lies more in normalizing relationships and opening the way for further assistance than in the face value of 'relief' that is offered."[59]

Treasury Secretary Paul O'Neill and Bono got a few tastes of the complications of implementing aid programs on their 2002 trip to Africa. O'Neill had long felt that aid was often "misused and [failed] to help" Africa. Before his trip, he noted that poor nations had received "trillions of dollars in aid over the years with precious little to show for it."[60] Still, he presented a plan to Ugandan President Yoweri Museveni to provide clean water to the entire country for $25 million. "It will cost many times your price," Museveni responded, citing a U.S. study with a $2 billion price tag. O'Neill looked at the study: "This is recommending you build a water system like in Detroit or Cleveland. You won't need that for a hundred years. You just need to drop wells, and mostly maintain them. Your people can handle the rest. We can do this quickly, maybe a year or two."[61] Yet nothing happened, and a few months later, the White House fired O'Neill.

On another occasion, Bono and O'Neill visited an enormous hospital that said it received $50 million yearly for AIDS, yet its HIV-positive mothers, who needed only $2 million, remained untreated. "This whole business about having so much money, and it not going primarily to treatment is just a stunning revelation," said O'Neill, his voice quivering.

"Before we ask for more money, for God's sake what are we doing with what we've got?"[62]

Bono responded to the charge that corruption deviates aid by agreeing but also proposing remedies. He read the work of Paul Theroux and others who argued that aid had worsened Africa's poverty. "I realized that a lot of the aid for instance had been incredibly badly mishandled over the years, creating worse situations. . . . Without strict conditionalities, there was no point in giving."[63] Yet he remained a believer:

> Aid, it's clear, is still part of the picture. It's crucial, if you have HIV and are fighting for your life, or if you are a mother wondering why you can't protect your child against killers with unpronounceable names or if you are a farmer who knows that new seed varietals will mean you have produce that you can take to market in drought or flood. But not the old, dumb only game in town aid—smart aid that aims to put itself out of business in a generation or two. "Make aid history" is the objective.[64]

But as Bono said in 2013, finance ministers had taught him that corruption was perhaps the most important impediment to development. Africans agreed. "It's very understandable for the developing world to cringe when aid is sort of waved around as a sort of . . . silver bullet. What they want to be able to do is look after their own destinies"[65]:

> If we see aid as investment, and the debt burden of these countries as unjust, and offer fairer trade conditions, Africa will be able to take charge of its own destiny. The reason for the T for Trade in DATA is, in the end, aid is not the way forward for the poorest people in the world. Trade is the way forward. We have to let the poorest of the poor trade with us. . . . I'm not for some sort of paternalistic attitude to Africa. I'm against it. But in order for that to happen, we have to break a certain chain.[66]

Bono trusted in the ability of the United Nations to "police and audit where the money is being spent." And under the Millennium Challenge Account, "countries would get a special grant if they really were serious about tackling poverty, and were open to criticism, encouraging civil society, a free press, etcetera." The Global Fund integrated oversight by giving two years of a grant up front, then assessing results, and then giving the last three years. Using that mechanism, the Global Fund pulled grants from Nigeria and withheld others from South Africa and Senegal. Some of Bono's remedies—access to global bond markets and fairer trade pacts—were exactly what Dambisa Moyo also preached.[67]

The corruption issue came up often with those in charge of aid. From one U.S. member of Congress, Bono heard, "You're not gonna get this money [for debt relief], because I know where it's going. It's going down a rat hole, these guys have been ripping us off for years. Because Africa's first problem is not natural calamity, it's not their corrupt relationship with Europe and America. They're the second and third problem. The first problem is their own corrupt leadership." Bono and his allies "convinced him that the money would be well spent, and later when I came back from Uganda, I took him pictures of a water hole. I said: 'There's the money. It didn't go do a rat hole, it went down a water hole, Congressman!'"[68]

A fifth and final set of criticisms had to do with the Western politicians who stood in the way of Bono's visions and aid getting to its intended recipients. For conservative administrations such as that of George W. Bush, PEPFAR's otherwise laudable $15 billion for AIDS relief came with strings: "1/3 of the prevention funds go to programs promoting abstinence and sexual fidelity, stringent restrictions on the use of condoms and even a demand that groups receiving funds must formally oppose prostitution," wrote Browne.[69]

Perhaps the most stinging argument is that politicians who promised aid but did not deliver it manipulated Bono and his ilk. There were precedents. In 1974, most industrialized nations had promised to dedicate 0.7 percent of their gross national product to global development, but 30 years later, they were donating only half that. In the same vein, the $100 billion promised to Jubilee in 1999 had produced only $36.3 billion in funds actually cleared by May 2003.[70]

On these last criticisms, Bono showed his steep learning curve and his courage in confronting donors. He was wary of the lack of follow-through by politicians and not afraid to denounce it. In 2004, he wrote to Bush that "while the [Millennium Challenge] office has been slow to open and money not out the door the way we'd like, the tough-but-fair approach is one that Americans, when they understand it, appreciate and applaud."[71]

Bono also publicly held specific politicians to their promises. In 2002–2004, Bono lobbied hard the Canadian administrations of Jean Chrétien and of his successor, Paul Martin. Thanks to Bono's efforts, the

2002 G8 meeting in Alberta was focused on Africa, and debt relief remained high on the Canadian foreign policy agenda. Bono even gave the keynote address at Martin's formal election as prime minister, praising the Canadian for being "a politician who doesn't break his promises."

In the same speech, Bono also warned, "I'm going to become the biggest pain of his life! Paul Martin thinks he likes me. He doesn't know what he signed on for—more lobbying about debt, begging for letters, petitions for unfair trade, phone calls about money for the global health fund." When Martin eventually did break his promise, Bono ranted on national Canadian radio, "I'm annoyed. I'm bewildered, really. I'm disappointed. I can't believe that Paul Martin would want to hold up history." He shared Martin's phone number with 18,000 fans at U2's Vancouver concert and asked them to call in with complaints.[72]

DATA similarly urged British Prime Minister Tony Blair not only to "talk the talk for Africa" but also to "walk the walk" in his budget. When numbers for the Millennium Challenge came in low, Bono expressed his dilemma: "I'm pissed, I'm mad in fact that not more has happened. . . . We have denounced the administration . . . but, we're not placarding and throwing rotten tomatoes at people who are trebling aid to Africa."[73]

When Bush proposed cuts to his own HIV/AIDS bill, DATA launched a Keep America's Promise to Africa campaign, which again enlisted Christian musicians and church leaders. Bono argued that an extra $1 billion in funding would prevent 1.6 million people from getting infected. And when an Iowa representative proposed other cuts, DATA played hardball, targeting his district with radio ads, letters to local newspapers, and "action alerts" that urged activists to flood his Washington office with calls. The Iowan relented, admitting that he had "heard from a number of Iowa constituents who were concerned about funding for international programs fighting AIDS and other diseases."[74]

Most frustrating to Bono was the slippage after the massive 2005 G8 promises. Two years after the pledges, DATA found that the seven wealthiest nations had increased aid by less than half of what was expected in order to double aid to Africa by 2010 as promised. DATA refused to count debt relief in its calculations and accused rich nations of overstating that relief. Bono accused the rich nations of "obfuscation." Bob Geldof called the work of the G8 "a total farce." By 2009, the United Kingdom was the only country to have honored its promises. He asked rhetorically of G8 leaders, "Do they think we can't read or count?"[75]

In June 2007 in Germany, Bono confronted Chancellor Angela Merkel. "We absolutely take you at your word, but if the others don't come through," he half threatened, "well, you know nothing creates cynics faster than when leaders accept applause for commitments they then fail to meet." He lectured, "To break a promise to the most vulnerable people on the planet is profane."

By 2009, Merkel had overdelivered, causing Bono a sigh of relief.[76]

Bono was not so successful with Silvio Berlusconi, Italy's notorious prime minister. Berlusconi admitted that he considered raising his country's aid to avoid a "tongue-lashing" from Bono. But in the end, the Italian *reduced* aid by over €200 million.[77]

Bono was most incensed at the failure of states to help with his "trade not aid" agenda. He long advocated justice in trade deals with Africa as a far more sustainable solution to poverty than charity. He criticized France, for example, for fearing the dismantling of the Common Agricultural Policy, which subsidized small European farmers and thus unfairly punished African competitors. But Bono remained patient, buoyed by past successes: "Look, we've made progress on debt and aid and that must be celebrated. Trade will be a long haul fight, an epic long term battle."[78]

By 2015, ONE still congratulated itself on "playing a crucial role in the G8's historic commitment in 2005 to double funding to fight poverty and disease in Africa—and holding their feet to the fire ever since."[79]

And Bono and his organizations were focused laser-like on results. "I've learned just to be an evidence-based activist," he once reflected. "Cut through the crap. Find out what works. Find out what doesn't work. I don't come from a hippie tradition of let's all hold hands and the world is going to be a better place. My thing's much more punk rock. I enjoy the math, actually. The math is incredible."[80]

He had many examples of math to choose from. Because of debt relief, Mozambique's payments were down 42 percent, freeing up $14 million for health. More doctors were getting supplies, more children were going to school, and measles cases were down.[81] "There is three times the amount of children going to school in Uganda now," he noted in 2004, "as the result of debt cancellation. That's just one country. All over the developing world, you'll find hospitals built with that money, real lives changed, communities transformed."[82] In one of his *New York Times* op-eds, he reported in 2009 that 34 million African children were now in school "in large part because their governments used money freed up by debt relief." "Providing AIDS medication to just under four million people, putting in place modest measures to improve maternal health, eradicating killer pests like malaria and rotoviruses—all these provide a leg up on the climb to self-sufficiency."[83] A few months later, Bono praised Ghana for its progress toward achieving Millennium Development Goals as well as the continent's growing middle class, its opportunities for investment and growth, and individual Africans who led accountability and anticorruption efforts. Bill Gates's goal was to reduce corruption not completely but to 5 percent of the aid given.[84]

For achieving these results, the Bill and Melinda Gates Foundation praised DATA as a great example of leveraging small budgets into large donations—"$50 billion in debt relief and aid for a $1 million investment." This results-oriented approach allegedly also inspired reforms at older philanthropies.[85]

A completely separate set of criticisms was aimed at Bono—and this time the rest of the band too—for their business practices.

This was an unprecedented line of attack because U2 were long admired for their business acumen and ethics. Unlike other bands, they had never squandered their earnings on vice, nor had they made disastrous business decisions. Instead, they reinvested almost all profits into the band's organization and tours. Early in their careers, U2 brilliantly negotiated to own all the rights to their back catalog, including a piece of Island Records, their recording company from the early 1980s. In 1989, when Polygram bought Island, U2's shares of the company netted them over £20 million, with allegedly tens of millions more in the 1990s.[86]

The wealth kept accumulating: in 2005, Bono was rumored to have amassed £50 million. In 2012 alone, the band made a $78 million profit from their 360 Tour, which grossed $736 million in its three years. When Facebook went public that same year, Bono made about $10 million—not the $1.5 billion rumored but a nice payday nonetheless.[87] By late 2013, the wealth of the band as a whole was estimated at $1.1 billion and Bono's at $600 million.[88] The following year, when it released *Songs of Innocence* on iTunes, Apple reportedly added $100 million to the band's coffers.

Many in the business world also admired their early investments in future technologies and ability to market the band without "selling out." U2 once turned down $23 million from a car company for the use of a song.[89] They also developed a relationship early on with Apple, becoming among the first adopters of iTunes, and in 2004 garnered global—and largely positive—attention for their exclusive U2 iPod and their new album by shilling for Apple's revolutionary product yet receiving no compensation. That relationship soured when Bono and Apple founder Steve Jobs had a falling out that included the words "go fuck yourself." The singer "had a tantrum, like a child," he recalled, "and went to the competition"—Blackberry—which sponsored their 360 Tour. Still, the deals kept coming. In 2008, U2 signed a 12-year deal with Live Nation worth about £50 million in which the entertainment giant would book U2's shows but also assume all risk during tours. In 2012, Bono and The Edge invested in Dropbox, an online file storage and sharing company.[90]

These were lucrative deals but not highly controversial. Bono and the boys drew more fire with other investments. In 2004, Bono joined the board of Elevation Partners, a new private equity firm that invested in media, entertainment, and technology. By 2014, it had $1.9 billion in its portfolio, which included Facebook, Forbes, Yelp, and Palm, among others, and commentators estimated Bono's share at about a fifth. Among the more unsavory products put out by the partners of Elevation Partners were video games called "Mercenaries 2: World in Flames" and "Destroy All Humans."[91]

Bono's response to investing in video games: "Am I as excited about this as I am for an AIDS vaccine? No, but there it is."[92]

Bono rejected any claims that rock stars should not also be shrewd business leaders. "I think there's a lot of baggage carried over from the sixties, that says a musician shouldn't be a businessman, because—hey man!—you're supposed to be out there, man, just smoking the weed, putting your toes in the river, surrounded by a bunch of beautiful girls combing your hair as you watch the sun come up."[93]

Bono also rationalized his immense wealth and the secrecy behind it. In 1989, he admitted that both the band's and each individual's wealth are kept "secret, and while that doesn't absolve us from all the guilt of having a lot of money in a society that doesn't have much, at least it makes us feel we're doing something worthwhile with that money." "From all the flak we get in this level from the middle class, we still have a huge working class audience. . . . There, I think people feel 'well, it's his business.' And they know we pay taxes and they know we make a lot of money for the country anyway. I mean, I don't mind paying taxes though I try to pay as little as I can, obviously."[94]

Given Bono's habit of telling governments how to spend tax money, cries of hypocrisy grew most strident when on June 1, 2006, the band moved their publishing royalties—one third of their income—out of Ireland and to the Netherlands to reduce their tax burden by half, just as the Rolling Stones had done for years. The move was a response to Ireland's new €250,000 cap on tax-free royalties for artists.[95] To *Hot Press*, U2's longtime champion in the Irish music press, McGuinness explained that "the reality is that U2's business is 90% conducted around the world. 90% of our tickets and 98% of our records are sold outside of Ireland. It's where we live and where we work and where we employ a lot of people. But we pay taxes all over the world—of many different kinds. And like any other business, we are perfectly entitled to minimise the tax we pay."[96] "We found ourselves paying a lot of tax instead of supporting new business," Bono further explained. "I would be reluctant to call it a strategy but it is more fun to develop new things than give the money to the government."[97] The Edge added that "our business is a very complex business. Of course we're trying to be tax-efficient. Who doesn't want to be tax-efficient?"

Critics pounced anyway. "The practical consequences of being 'tax-efficient' are many," wrote a commentator. "If you say you care about Africa, why are you paying fees to international money movers who encourage Africa's 'tax-efficient' kleptomaniacs to hide their loot in tax havens? You are also forcing fellow citizens, who didn't make U2's estimated $110m in 2005, to pick up the bill, not only for foreign aid, but for education, health, law and order and defence." Monbiot of *The Guardian* found Bono's preaching transparency to corporations "revolting" because of the singer's own refusal to reveal his business dealings.[98]

As usual, the Irish were most acerbic. Irish-born comedian Graham Norton was typical: "People like Bono really annoy me. He goes to hell and back to avoid paying tax. He has a special accountant. He works out Irish tax loopholes. And then he's asking me to buy a well for an African village. Tarmac a road or pay for a school, you tight-wad!" Even Social Protection Minister Joan Burton cited U2 as a "not acceptable" example of how "a huge amount of personal wealth and corporate earnings and corporate profits are diverted in a way in which they make little effective contribution" and hurt public services.[99]

A group of protesters called Art Uncut hit where it hurt most—Bono's work for the poor of the world: "Bono claims to care about the developing world, but U2 greedily indulges in the very kind of tax avoidance that is crippling poor nations." A coalition of 70 groups added that "tax avoidance and tax evasion costs the impoverished world at least $160m (£142.5m) every year. This is money urgently required to bring people out of poverty." The global recession that hit Ireland particularly hard by 2009 redoubled the anger, with Art Uncut arguing that "tax nestling in the band's bank account should be helping to keep open the hospitals, schools and libraries that are closing all over Ireland" (see figure 5.3). [100]

None of these critics accused U2 of anything illegal. A BBC investigative program confirmed the band's business honesty. One tax analyst, praising U2 as "global citizens" who had a right to be "financially smart," pointed out that the band's move to Holland shut down no factories and killed no job. [101]

In 2007, Bono further defended the band. "Our tax has always been not just to the letter of the law but to the spirit of the law," he said. "This country's prosperity came out of tax innovation so it would be sort of churlish to criticize U2 for what we were encouraged to do and what brought all of these companies in the first place." In 2013, he reiterated that U2's practices were in "total harmony with our government's philosophy" of low taxes, adding that he nevertheless understood the annoyance of the "cranky left." [102] He elsewhere expanded on U2's role in developing Ireland: "The rise out of despair of the 60s and 70s that I was born into would not have happened without investment by American companies: Intel, Microsoft, Dell. A lot of us badgered our friends at Google to set up their offices outside of America in Dublin and they did. As did Facebook. And they're pleased they did." Irish journalist Niall Stokes added that Bono "has been hugely instrumental in encouraging the clustering of companies in the tech sector here, which now employs over 110,000 people." [103]

Figure 5.3.   An anti-U2 placard at the Glastonbury Festival in England, June 24, 2011. The placard referred to U2 pulling out of the previous year's festival because of Bono's back injury but was also a reference to protests at the festival against U2's tax avoidance. *Adrian Sherratt Photography Ltd/REX USA*

Still, the resentment over U2's activism, some of it misplaced, led some to wallow in recriminations. One financial website, for example, saw Bono as a hypocrite for denouncing oil corporations' "tax avoidance," when in reality he criticized their lack of transparency—two completely different issues.[104] Questions about taxes dogged U2 for years after the 2006 move.

* * *

"I don't have to live up to people's expectations of who they think I should be," Bono ruminated at the beginning of the second half of the 2000s.[105] But it was clear that public expectations always mattered for celebrities since it was the currency they traded in return for money or power. And if Bono wanted tremendous amounts of money from those in power for the poorest and least powerful in the world, his image needed to remain beyond reproach. The evolution of U2's global activism in the twenty-first century would continue to depend on this balancing act.

CONCLUSION

Of Fans and Activists

U2 and Bono have impacted how I see the world and what I am willing to consider doing in order to bring about change . . . or at least do my part.—Jennifer, U2 fan and activist[1]

Criticism against U2 and Bono for their activism has been at times envious, petty, irrelevant, or cynical. At other times, however, it has denoted a healthy, useful skepticism about celebrity lobbying, about paternalism and hypocrisy, and especially about the assumed impact of development aid.

But while many have argued against the band's having improved the developing world, few have questioned U2's good intentions and even its leadership in reshaping activism in the modern world. U2 has been at the forefront of major trends in politicizing music in the last 40 years—the focus on human rights, the turn to direct action and involvement in political campaigns, the lobbying on behalf of highly indebted nations and against disease, and especially the transformation of philanthropy into a permanent, institutionalized part of Western politics. Throughout its nearly four decades as an international act, U2 and its audiences have fought a noble struggle "to figure out how to live in this world," as The Edge said, even as that world became ever more selfish and U2's activism became a symptom of that selfishness.

Those audiences need to be celebrated not only for their own good works—works that give hope that the world may not be so selfish after all—but also because their own struggles for peace and justice help demonstrate the real impact of U2 in the world. What most delighted me in reading about the band was the discovery that I was not alone in seeing U2 as an inspiration for what was, for me, a temporary but fulfilling experience of leading an Amnesty International group while still a teenager in the 1980s. My story has been relived thousands of times.

In the 1980s, U2's status as the Biggest Band in the World gave a green light for fans to put into practice what they heard in U2's music and especially at its live shows, at which Bono regularly discussed social and political issues. *Time* magazine declared, "It is no longer corny or uncool to be concerned, to get involved. . . . Audiences are ready to take heart and to reach out."[2]

Reach out they did. "What U2 says is what we want to be" is how Laurie Wong, a 17-year-old from California, justified her transformation in 1987 from fan to activist. Wong attended a monthly meeting called A Celebration, in a Hollywood nightclub of all places, where admission fees made their way to Amnesty International and World Vision. The cofounders had met at a U2 concert a few years before, organizing get-togethers at which attendees brought cans of food for the homeless. "Cynics say, 'I can't change the world,'" said one cofounder. "I can't change the world, but I can change the world for one person. . . . That's the idealism we believe in. That's what U2 said all along. This is right. This is true."[3]

Tour after tour convinced Bono of the ability to create activism out of the emotional commitment that U2 garnered from its audiences. "Sometimes people go to a concert, any concert, and they're nervous. . . . The tension is still there at the end when people walk out. A U2 concert seems to be different and that's the healing thing, the washing thing." He conceded that emotions could disappear right after the concert. "But there's unity for an hour and a half, musicians can do what politicians can't do and I think those feelings, those communal feelings are quite addictive."[4]

U2 realized that modern-day concertgoers, especially young ones, attended largely for the sense of community and unity that they brought. And once that community was solidified, it could move en masse. After *The Joshua Tree* came out, Bono said that "the goal of all U2 songs" was "to inspire people to think for themselves." Reflecting on the complacent age he lived in, he added, "We are in a big sleep, where I'm okay, you're okay. And we don't ask questions that have difficult answers. And if U2 is throwing cold water over that kind of thinking and people are wak-ing—that's fine."[5]

Over the years, many have studied whether U2's music and activism really motivated others to become activists. In 1997, while the band played in Sarajevo after the siege, one researcher monitored chatter on "Wire," an unofficial U2 e-mail list. He found that, "at its worst," the list was "a playground for the most powerful: educated White males with lots of free time." But "at its most idealistic, Wire is an environment that welcomes and encourages multiple global cultures and discourses—an exemplar of the most utopian visions of the Internet." By 2009, fans had created hundreds of unofficial websites.[6]

In 2004 and 2005, another scholar interviewed 70 U2 fans from doz-ens of countries. All admired Bono for his activism. Fifty-three said that U2 had an impact or at least an indirect influence on how they saw the world, although few became full-blown activists. Jennifer was not that atypical: "There are so many issues I had not been informed of until Bono and/or U2 brought them to my attention. I don't believe in everything Bono believes in, but his opinion does count big time with me. Have his actions made me act in turn? Yes. I have been a member of Greenpeace and Amnesty International since '87. I am extremely active with Amnes-ty."[7]

Yet another scholar, Rachel Seiler, collected stories of "the relation-ship between U2's music and listeners' progressive awareness—the mar-riage of critical consciousness and action for social justice and change"—and wove them into a composite interviewee. "I would not be the person I am today if I had not encountered the music. U2 completely catapulted me to adulthood," revealed that composite, describing U2's music and lyrics as "little seeds" that grew into "plants inside of me. That's what we're put on this place for; it's not about this consume, consume, con-sume, buy more stuff, grow the economy, blah, blah, blah. No, we are here to meet other people's needs." Getting more specific, it said, "'Pride' was definitely my introduction to Martin Luther King, which was my introduction to racial injustice. My apologies to my former history profes-sors, but it wasn't until U2 that I really became aware of the history of US involvement in Central America."[8]

Hope, community, and faith came back again and again as results of listening to U2:

When I listen to the music, I'm encouraged. I mean, it's one of those top, top things in my life that provides stability, a point of reference, a foundation for me. . . . So the first time I saw U2, I would say I had a spiritual experience. The audience was almost like an organism. . . . Ecofeminists would say that there's a unity of experience where you have. . . . I felt a connection, a greater connection beyond myself. . . . I go to church and I love the people in my church, but I . . . yeah . . . seeing U2 feels more like church. . . . I think that U2 fans really and truly are different form fans of, you know, whoever—pick an artist; we're probably more politically aware and more likely to be active in personal acts of engagement. There's something we identify in one another; there is kind of this feeling of equality, camaraderie, holding one another accountable and caring for one another—like a huge family of different ages and stages of development everybody is affected by everybody.

Seiler concluded that "U2 culture fills the roles of a community as outlined by West African elder Malidoma Some: a healthy sense of belonging; an outlet for natural abilities; and a recognition that the needs of the one are the needs of the many, not the needs of the one over the needs of the many."[9]

Fans especially refuted a charge leveled at U2 by the uninitiated—that they were merely sloganeering and preaching to empty-headed sheep. "They do not tell you what to think—they want you to come along for the ride and to do what you think is socially responsible," said fans. "Through U2, I very quickly was able to find the kind of organization that would be my home—specifically, Amnesty International." Seiler noted "five compelling themes" in "the profile of a conscious listener": "consciousness raising," "values," "enhancing connections," "meaningful being," and "action." "U2 supports them to think autonomously and reflexively in ways that challenge habitual modes and reveal systems of oppression and injustice." "The participants describe U2's music as being and speaking deep truth, and they suggest that the spiritual element of the music and of themselves is inseparable from the spiritual element of justice work and the need for justice in the world."[10]

A 2013 Australian film titled *Meet Me in the Sound* documented how U2's music touched its fans, helping them deal with spirituality, depression, poverty, and child abuse. That same year, when Bono hurt his back, an eight-year-old from Canada called Nathaniel set up a Facebook page in order to send letters and cards to the singer.[11]

Bono would be charmed by such stories, believing as he does that music is a conductor of positive energy among a community and a driver of charitable action mediated by faith. Music "can help to change things, not in any melodramatic way, but certainly as part of a movement of positive protest," he once said[12]:

> You see things going on out there and you think, "Well, what the hell can I do about it?" For a lot of people there's not a lot you can do about it and all I believe is that everyone in their own way has a position they have to take and if that's as a mother with snotty nosed kids or a guy in a factory just doing the best he can or being a schoolteacher or a farmer, you just find your ground, your place and you just do the best you can to shine a light on the s**t that's out there. . . . I'm in a band and I just hope that when it's all over for U2 that in some way we've made the light a bit brighter. Maybe just tore off a corner of the darkness.[13]

Episcopal priest Beth Maynard offered a reasonable counter to trying to measure U2's impact on fans. "There is no way ever to quantify how many audience members would cite something they saw or heard at a U2 show as a factor in their subsequent decisions to donate, lobby, volunteer, join Amnesty International, or explore a vocation in ministry or social work or development. However, the number is surely not negligible."[14]

What is also not negligible is that most whose lives were changed by U2—toward more compassion, sharper convictions, stronger faith, or more direct activism—were often first touched by the music as teenagers. Journalism professor David Hajdu suggested that 14 "is a formative age, especially for people growing up in social contexts framed by pop culture. You're in the ninth grade, confronting the tyrannies of sex and adulthood, struggling to figure out what kind of adult you'd like to be, and you turn to the cultural products most important in your day as sources of cool—the capital of young life." For 14-year-olds, chief among those cultural products is music.[15] Seiler confirms about her interviewees that "adolescence was the time in the participants' lives when they had their first and most vivid experiences at the intersection of music, sociopolitical thought, and action and their emerging identity."[16] I was also 14 when I went to my first U2 concert. If I encountered U2's music today, I'd probably be more critical of them. But I'm glad I didn't.

U2, of course, are no longer teenagers. They are in the mid-fifties. Are we seeing U2 enter the last stage of its life as a band, as activists? Their geographical expansion alone might indicate that they have nowhere else to go. After all, in the last decades they have grown out of Ireland into Europe, then America, then the world, now touring regularly in every large city on the globe with a stadium. The "outer space" theme of their 2009–2011 tour—the intro was David Bowie's "Space Oddity" and their outro Elton John's "Rocket Man"—suggested that they had perhaps grown beyond the Biggest Band in the World to now be the Biggest Band in the Universe.[17] Their November 2014 *Rolling Stone* cover was titled, unsurprisingly, "U2 Take on the World," as if to suggest that their wing-span could not be shorter.[18]

In a way, U2 and space is not such a strange pairing. Bono once said that the band began "with its roots in space somewhere," indicating its lack of roots.[19] And the space motif, prevalent also in videos and magazine covers, was not new in 2009. The Zoo TV tour in the early 1990s introduced the "Spacebaby" animation, suggesting innocent souls adrift in a postmodern cosmos.[20]

But the world is actually a fitting descriptor for what has become U2's community. The final word should go to writer Anthony DeCurtis, who knows the band personally and speaks to the unlimited potential they have unleashed among not only fans but all activists as well: "Their music, even the beautiful, ghostly atmospherics of *No Line on the Horizon*, continues to be a call to action in the world and action in the fertile realms of our imaginations. . . . There truly is no line on the horizon—no line between Earth and sky, between young and old, between the fates of the poorest and the richest, between who we are and who we aspire to be."[21]

NOTES

INTRODUCTION

1. John Hutchinson, "Luminous Times: U2 Wrestle with Their Moment of Glory," reproduced in Hank Bordowitz, *The U2 Reader: A Quarter Century of Commentary, Criticism, and Reviews* (Milwaukee, WI: Hal Leonard, 2003), 65.

2. On U2's implicit feminism, see Jennifer McClinton-Temple and Abigail Myers, "U2, Feminism, and Ethics of Care," in *U2 and Philosophy: How to Decipher an Atomic Band*, ed. Mark A. Wrathall (Chicago: Open Court, 2006), 109–22.

3. Laura Jackson, *Bono: His Life, Music, and Passions* (New York: Citadel Press, 2003), 78.

4. Todd McFlicker notes many other similarities in *All You Need Is Love to Dismantle an Atomic Bomb: How the Beatles and U2 Changed the World* (New York: Continuum, 2007).

5. Brian Hiatt, "Trying to Throw Their Arms around the World," *Rolling Stone*, November 6, 2014, 57.

6. John Waters, *Race of Angels: The Genesis of U2* (London: Fourth Estate, 1994), 287–88.

7. Greg Garrett, *We Get to Carry Each Other: The Gospel According to U2* (Louisville, KY: Westminster John Knox Press, 2009), 88.

8. James Traub, "The Statesman," *New York Times Magazine*, September 18, 2005, 80ff.

9. "U2 Charity Work, Events and Causes," www.looktothestars.org/celebrity/u2, and "Bono Charity Work, Events and Causes," www.looktothestars.org/celebrity/bono, both accessed February 9, 2015.

10. Raymond Chegedua Tangonyire Achal, SJ, and Lawrence Kyaligonza, SJ, *Economic Behaviour As If Others Too Had Interests* (Bamenda, Cameroon: Langaa RPCIG, 2012).

11. Joshua Karliner, *The Corporate Planet: Ecology and Politics in the Age of Globalization* (San Francisco: Sierra Club Books, 1997), 1–25; see also Robert H. Frank, *Luxury Fever: Money and Happiness in an Era of Excess* (Princeton, NJ: Princeton University Press, 1999), 33–44.

12. Michael J. Sandel, *What Money Can't Buy: The Moral Limits of Markets* (New York: Farrar, Straus and Giroux, 2012), 6–8.

13. Elena Pulcini, *Care of the World: Fear, Responsibility, and Justice in the Global Age*, trans. Karen Whittle (New York: Springer, 2013), 19, 4–7.

14. To be sure, terms like "narcissism," "selfishness," and "egoism" are not equal. Some are more clinical; others can have positive attributes. But all denote an increased self-centeredness in modern society.

15. Christopher Lasch, *The Culture of Narcissism* (New York: Norton, 1979); Charles Taylor, *The Ethics of Authenticity* (Cambridge, MA: Harvard University Press, 1992).

16. Lynne Malcolm, "Research Says Young People Today Are More Narcissistic Than Ever," *All in the Mind*, May 16, 2014, www.abc.net.au/radionational/programs/allinthemind/young-people-today-are-more-narcissistic-than-ever/5457236, accessed November 7, 2014; Sadie F. Dingfelder, "Reflecting on Narcissism: Are Young People More Self-Obsessed Than Ever Before?," *Monitor on Psychology* 42, no. 2 (February 2011), www.apa.org/monitor/2011/02/narcissism.aspx, accessed November 7, 2014; Jean M. Twenge and W. Keith Campbell, *The Narcissism Epidemic: Living in the Age of Entitlement* (New York: Atria, 2009), 2, 17, 259–79.

17. Robert Putnam, *Bowling Alone: The Collapse and Revival of American Community* (New York: Simon & Schuster, 2000).

18. Mark R. Reiff, *Exploitation and Economic Justice in the Liberal Capitalist State* (New York: Oxford University Press, 2013), 5–10; Annie Lowry, "The Wealth Gap in America Is Growing, Too," *New York Times*, April 2, 2014, http://economix.blogs.nytimes.com/2014/04/02/the-wealth-gap-is-growing-too/?_php=true&_type=blogs&_r=0, accessed April 23, 2014.

19. Relative, that is, to the rich world when the rich world was at a similar stage of development.

20. Alastair Greig, David Hulme, and Mark Turner, *Challenging Global Inequality: Development Theory and Practice in the 21st Century* (New York: Palgrave Macmillan, 2007), 2.

21. Dan Brockington, *Celebrity Advocacy and International Development* (New York: Routledge, 2014), 18.

22. See, for example, Branko Milanovic, *Worlds Apart: Measuring International and Global Inequality* (Princeton, NJ: Princeton University Press, 2005), 79–81.

23. Tangonyire and Achal, *Economic Behaviour As If Others Too Had Interests*, 73–78.

24. Frank, *Luxury Fever*, 38–39.

25. Jeffrey D. Sachs, *Common Wealth: Economics for a Crowded Planet* (New York: Penguin, 2008), 5.

26. J. C. Sevcik, "The US Is Not a Democracy but an Oligarchy, Study Concludes," United Press International, April 16, 2014, www.upi.com/Top_News/US/2014/04/16/The-US-is-not-a-democracy-but-an-oligarchy-study-concludes/2761397680051, accessed April 21, 2014.

27. "Stop the Madness," interview with Rupert Cornwell, *Globe and Mail*, July 6, 2002.

28. Scott Calhoun, "Introduction," in *Exploring U2: Is This Rock 'n' Roll? Essays on the Music, Work, and Influence of U2* (Lanham, MD: Scarecrow Press, 2012), xxvi.

29. For the state of this literature, see Scott Calhoun, "Where Could We Go from Here? The State of U2 Studies," *Books and Culture*, November/December 2009, 14–15, and Calhoun, "Introduction," xxiii–xxvii. Calhoun organized the first- and second-ever conferences about the band in 2009 and 2013. The first, "U2: The Hype and the Feedback," at North Carolina Central University in Durham, resulted in Calhoun, *Exploring U2*. Information on the second can be found at http://U2conference.com/u2con-2013, accessed April 17, 2014.

30. For example, see Bono, "Introduction," in *Selections from the Book of Psalms* (New York: Grove Press, 1999), vii–xii; Raewynne J. Whiteley and Beth Maynard, eds., *Get Up Off Your Knees: Preaching the U2 Catalog* (Cambridge, MA: Cowley Publications, 2003); Steve Stockman, *Walk On: The Spiritual Journey of U2* (Orlando, FL: Relevant Books, 2005); Robert Vagacs, *Religious Nuts, Political Fanatics: U2 in Theological Perspective* (Eugene, OR: Cascade Books, 2005); Christian Scharen, *One Step Closer: Why U2 Matters to Those Seeking God* (Grand Rapids, MI: Brazos Press, 2006); Chad E. Seales, "Burned over Bono: U2's Rock 'n' Roll Messiah and His Religious Politic," *Journal of Religion and Popular Culture* 14, no. 1 (2006): n.p.; and Garrett, *We Get to Carry Each Other*. See also Beth Maynard's "U2 sermons," http://U2sermons.blogspot.com, accessed April 17, 2014.

31. See *Achtung! The U2 Studies Journal*, whose editors are Scott Calhoun and Arlan Elizabeth Hess of Washington & Jefferson College; Steven Quinn, "U2 and the Performance of (a Numb) Resistance," *Social Semiotics* 9, no. 1 (1999): 67–83; John Street, "Bob, Bono and Tony B: The Popular Artist as Politician," *Media, Culture and Society* 24 (2002): 433–41; Bordowitz, *The U2*

Reader; Wrathall, *U2 and Philosophy*; Douglas K. Blount, "Rattle and Film: U2, Nietzsche and Salvation in the Blues," in *Faith, Film and Philosophy: Big Ideas on the Big Screen*, ed. R. Douglas Geivett and James S. Spiegel (Downers Grove, IL: InterVarsity Press, 2007), 241–57; Kevin Holm-Hudson, "Et Tu, U2? 'Wake Up Dead Man' and Bono's Perceived Betrayal of the Faith," *Journal of Religion and Popular Culture* 16, no. 2 (2007): n.p.; Lynn Ramert, "A Century Apart: The Personality Performances of Oscar Wilde in the 1890s and U2's Bono in the 1990s," *Popular Music and Society* 32, no. 4 (2009): 447–60; and Calhoun, *Exploring U2*.

32. See, for example, Christin Dirchfield, *Bono* (Ann Arbor, MI: Cherry Lake Publishing, 2008), and Kim Washburn, *Breaking Through by Grace: The Bono Story* (Grand Rapids, MI: Zonderkidz, 2010).

33. Nathan Jackson has produced the very competent *Bono's Politics: The Future of Celebrity Political Activism* (Saarbrücken: VDM Verlag Dr. Müller, 2008), but it was self-published and therefore remained obscure. Its topic is also limited to Bono and the model of activism he represents. In 2013, Irish journalist Harry Browne published *The Frontman: Bono (In the Name of Power)* (London: Verso), an attack on Bono as a hypocrite and pawn of global economic elites. Among articles on Bono is Andrew Cooper, "Beyond One Image Fits All: Bono and the Complexity of Celebrity Diplomacy," *Global Governance: A Review of Multilateralism and International Organizations* 14, no. 3 (July–September 2008): 265–72.

34. A similar but longer list of "eight permanent features," or U2's "genetic code," is in Višnja Cogan, *U2: An Irish Phenomenon* (Cork: The Collins Press, 2006), 6. They are community, Irishness, the creative process, spirituality, ambition, social consciousness, image and myth, and fans.

35. Cogan, *U2*, 29.

36. Cited in Waters, *Race of Angels*, 71.

37. Noel McLaughlin, "Bono! Do You Ever Take Those Wretched Sunglasses Off? U2 and the Performance of Irishness," *Popular Music History* 4, no. 3 (2009): 309.

38. Cited in Robert Hilburn, "U2: At Home in Dublin," *Los Angeles Times*, April 12, 1987, http://articles.latimes.com/1987-04-12/entertainment/ca-828_1_u2-album, accessed April 17, 2014.

39. Scharen, *One Step Closer*, 183.

40. Cogan, *U2*, 30.

41. Michael Stallard, "3 Practices CEOs Should Adopt from This Rock Star," Fox Business, January 9, 2014, www.foxbusiness.com/business-leaders/2014/01/09/3-practices-ceos-should-adopt-from-this-rock-star, accessed April 14, 2014.

42. Browne, *The Frontman*, 2.

43. Much of the ideas and the literature of cosmopolitanism are summarized in Karen Hendershot and Jill Sperandio, "Study Abroad and Development of Global Citizen Identity and Cosmopolitan Ideals in Undergraduates," *Current Issues in Comparative Education* 12, no. 1 (2009): 45–55.

44. Kwame Anthony Appiah, *Cosmopolitanism: Ethics in a World of Strangers* (New York: Norton, 2006), xiv, xv. On cosmopolitanism and global citizenship, see also Michael Karlberg, "Discourse, Identity, and Global Citizenship," *Peace Review* 20, no. 3 (2008): 310–20; Christopher Pallas, "Identity, Individualism, and Activism beyond the State: Examining the Impacts of Global Citizenship," *Global Society: Journal of Interdisciplinary International Relations* 26, no. 2 (2012): 169–89; and Florian Pichler, "Cosmopolitanism in a Global Perspective: An International Comparison of Open-Minded Orientations and Identity in Relation to Globalization," *International Sociology* 27, no. 1 (2012): 21–50.

45. Waters, *Race of Angels*, 67, 68.

46. Cited in Waters, *Race of Angels*, 127. See also Gerry Smyth, "'Show Me the Way to Go Home': Space and Place in the Music of U2," Space and the Irish Cultural Imagination (New York: Palgrave, 2001): 159–87.

47. Paul Hewson, "Bono: The White Nigger," in *Across the Frontiers: Ireland in the 1990s—Cultural, Political, Economic*, ed. Richard Kearney (Dublin: Wolfhound Press, 1989), 188.

48. Hewson, "Bono," 189.

49. Cited in Waters, *Race of Angels*, 128.

50. Waters, *Race of Angels*, 132.

51. Kerry Soper, "The Importance of Being Bono: The Philosophy and Politics of Identity in the Lyrics and Personae of U2's Frontman," in Wrathall, *U2 and Philosophy*, 56.

52. Cited in Wrathall, *U2 and Philosophy*, 58.

53. Cited in Beth Maynard, "Lent, Part One," in Whiteley and Maynard, *Get Up Off Your Knees*, 133.

54. Cited in *U2: The Ultimate Compendium of Interviews, Articles, Facts, and Opinions from the Files of* Rolling Stone (New York: Hyperion, 1994), xv.

55. Garrett, *We Get to Carry Each Other*, 18, 86.

56. Raewynne Whiteley, "There a Heavyness in the Air . . . ," in Whiteley and Maynard, *Get Up Off Your Knees*, 4, 5.

57. Cited in Waters, *Race of Angels*, 243, 244.

58. Garrett, *We Get to Carry Each Other*, 87.

59. Eugene Peterson, "Foreword," in Whiteley and Maynard, *Get Up Off Your Knees*, xi, xii, xiv.

60. "Transcript: Bono Remarks at the National Prayer Breakfast," *USA Today*, February 2, 2006, http://usatoday30.usatoday.com/news/washington/2006-02-02-bono-transcript_x.htm?POE=click-refer, accessed April 18, 2014.

61. Clint McCann, "Grace: U2, the Apostle Paul, and Latin American Theology," in Whiteley and Maynard, *Get Up Off Your Knees*, 61.

62. *The Charlie Rose Show*, May 16, 2013, www.atu2.com/news/video-bonos-interview-with-charlie-rose.html, accessed April 18, 2014.

63. Cited in David Fricke, "U2 Dissect 'Bomb,'" *Rolling Stone*, December 15, 2004, www.u2eastlink.com/foro/read.php?18,1000196817,1000196867, accessed April 18, 2014.

64. Cited in Stockman, *Walk On*, 190.

1. OUT OF IRELAND, 1960–1982

1. James Henke, "The Edge: The Rolling Stone Interview," *Rolling Stone*, March 10, 1987, www.atu2.com/news/the-edge-the-rolling-stone-interview.html, accessed November 10, 2014.

2. Eamon Dunphy, *Unforgettable Fire: The Story of U2* (London: Viking, 1987), 13–15.

3. Mick Wall, *Bono: In the Name of Love* (New York: Thunder's Mouth Press, 2005), 23.

4. Laura Jackson, *Bono: His Life, Music, and Passions* (New York: Citadel Press, 2003), 4.

5. Bill Flanagan, *U2 at the End of the World* (New York: Dell, 1995), 17.

6. Bono and Michka Assayas, *Bono* (New York: Riverhead Books, 2005), 11, 19, 16; *U2: The Ultimate Compendium of Interviews, Articles, Facts, and Opinions from the Files of* Rolling Stone (New York: Hyperion, 1994), 81.

7. Bono and Assayas, *Bono*, 15, 18.

8. Harry Browne, *The Frontman: Bono (In the Name of Power)* (London: Verso, 2013), 11.

9. Bono, liner notes, *Songs of Innocence*.

10. Wall, *Bono*, 23.

11. Neil McCormick, "Boy to Man: A Dublin-Shaped Band," in *Exploring U2: Is This Rock 'n' Roll? Essays on the Music, Work, and Influence of U2*, ed. Scott Calhoun (Lanham, MD: Scarecrow Press, 2012), 8.

12. *U2: The Ultimate Compendium*, 81.

13. John Waters, *Race of Angels: The Genesis of U2* (London: Fourth Estate, 1994), 33.

14. Bono, *Bono: In His Own Words* (New York: Omnibus Press, 1997), 33.

15. Carter, Alan, *U2: Wide Awake in America—12 Years with U2 Backstage and Beyond* (London: Boxtree, 1992), 52.

16. McCormick, "Boy to Man," 9.

17. Višnja Cogan, *U2: An Irish Phenomenon* (Cork: The Collins Press, 2006), 49.

18. *U2: The Ultimate Compendium*, 82.

19. Chris Heath, "Once upon a Time . . . ," reproduced in *The U2 Reader: A Quarter Century of Commentary, Criticism, and Reviews*, ed. Hank Bordowitz (Milwaukee, WI: Hal Leonard, 2003), 29.

20. *U2: The Ultimate Compendium*, 83; Waters, *Race of Angels*, 43.

21. Browne, *The Frontman*, 15.

22. McCormick, "Boy to Man," 9.

23. Dunphy, *Unforgettable Fire*, 12.

24. McCormick, "Boy to Man," 8.

25. Dunphy, *Unforgettable Fire*, 24.

26. "You cannot overstate the importance of the school in the incubation, nurturing, and flourishing of U2," wrote Neil McCormick in "Boy to Man," 11.

27. "Boy to Man," 12.

28. Wall, *Bono*, 46; McCormick, "Boy to Man," 11.

29. Paulo Hewitt, "Getting into U2," reproduced in Bordowitz, *The U2 Reader*, 5.

30. McCormick, "Boy to Man," 12.

31. Browne, *The Frontman*, 12.

32. McCormick, "Boy to Man," 5.

33. Jackson, *Bono*, 11.

34. "U2's Bono Speaks at GU Global Social Enterprise Event," November 12, 2012, www.georgetown.edu/webcast/bono-social-enterprise.html, accessed November 10, 2014.

35. Bono, liner notes, *Songs of Innocence*.

36. *U2: The Ultimate Compendium*, 92, xiv.

37. Jackson, *Bono*, 16.

38. Cited in *U2: The Ultimate Compendium*, 14.

39. Cited in Cogan, *U2*, 138.

40. Niall Stokes, *U2: The Stories behind Every U2 Song* (London: Carlton, 2009), 26.

41. Steve Stockman, *Walk On: The Spiritual Journey of U2* (Orlando, FL: Relevant Books, 2005), 15.

42. U2 and Neil McCormick, *U2 by U2* (New York: HarperCollins, 2006), 20.

43. Dunphy, *Unforgettable Fire*, 149–50.

44. Cited in Bono and Assayas, *Bono*, 136.

45. Heath, "Once upon a Time," 31, 32.

46. Cited in Bono and Assayas, *Bono*, 136.

47. Cited in U2 and McCormick, *U2 by U2*, 120.

48. Bono and Assayas, *Bono*, 163.

49. Bono and Friday, cited in Waters, *Race of Angels*, 41.

50. For more on this "spatial imagination at work," see Gerry Smyth, "'Show Me the Way to Go Home': Space and Place in the Music of U2," in *Space and the Irish Cultural Imagination*, (New York: Palgrave, 2001), 167.

51. Edwin Miller, "Rocking with U2," reproduced in Bordowitz, *The U2 Reader*, 27.

52. Both cited in *U2: The Ultimate Compendium*, 34, 31.

53. Bono and Assayas, *Bono*, 127, 133.

54. Bono, cited in *The U2 File: A Hot Press U2 History, 1978–1985*, ed. Niall Stokes (London: Omnibus Press, 1985), 32, 31.

55. Cited in *U2: The Ultimate Compendium*, 9–10, 2.

56. Dunphy, *Unforgettable Fire*, 92–94.

57. McCormick, "Boy to Man," 10, 15.

58. Dunphy, *Unforgettable Fire*, 130.

59. Jackson, *Bono*, 32.

60. Greg Garrett, *We Get to Carry Each Other: The Gospel According to U2* (Louisville, KY: Westminster John Knox Press, 2009), 5.

61. Both cited in *U2: The Ultimate Compendium*, 14, 16.

2. THE RAISING OF A GLOBAL CONSCIOUSNESS, 1983–1989

1. James Henke, "The Edge: The Rolling Stone Interview," *Rolling Stone*, March 10, 1987, www.atu2.com/news/the-edge-the-rolling-stone-interview.html, accessed November 10, 2014.

2. Adam Block, "Pure Bono (Part 1)," *Mother Jones Magazine*, May 1, 1989, www.atu2.com/news/pure-bono-part-1.html, accessed November 10, 2014.

3. Carter Alan, *U2: Wide Awake in America—12 Years with U2 Backstage and Beyond* (London: Boxtree, 1992), 131.

4. Jann S. Wenner, "Bono: The Rolling Stone Interview," *Rolling Stone*, November 3, 2005, 58.

5. Liam Mackey, "Articulate Speech of the Heart," *Hot Press*, August 5, 1983, www.hotpress.com/archive/549220.html, accessed November 10, 2014.

6. Cited in Henke, "The Edge."

7. On "New Year's Day" and the Solidarity movement, see Marina Berzins McCoy, "'We Can Be One': Love and Platonic Transcendence in U2," in *U2 and*

Philosophy: How to Decipher an Atomic Band, ed. Mark A. Wrathall (Chicago: Open Court, 2006), 3–14.

8. Bono, *Bono: In His Own Words* (New York: Omnibus Press, 1997), 44.

9. *U2: The Ultimate Compendium of Interviews, Articles, Facts, and Opinions from the Files of* Rolling Stone (New York: Hyperion, 1994), 13.

10. Bono and Michka Assayas, *Bono* (New York: Riverhead Books, 2005), 190.

11. Bono, "In Ireland, Tuesday's Grace," *New York Times*, June 19, 2010.

12. Laura Jackson, *Bono: His Life, Music, and Passions* (New York: Citadel Press, 2003), 43.

13. Cited in John Waters, *Race of Angels: The Genesis of U2* (London: Fourth Estate, 1994), 129, 186.

14. Mackey, "Articulate Speech of the Heart."

15. Nathan Dwayne Jackson, *Bono's Politics: The Future of Celebrity Political Activism* (Saarbrücken: VDM Verlag Dr. Müller, 2008), 28.

16. Bono and Assayas, *Bono*, 237.

17. Eamon Dunphy, *Unforgettable Fire: The Story of U2* (London: Viking, 1987), 172.

18. Mick Wall, *Bono: In the Name of Love* (New York: Thunder's Mouth Press, 2005), 123.

19. "The World about Us," in *U2: Three Chords and the Truth*, ed. Niall Stokes (New York: Harmony Books, 1989), 68, 70.

20. Cited in "Articulate Speech of the Heart," in *The U2 File: A Hot Press U2 History, 1978–1985*, ed. Niall Stokes (London: Omnibus, 1985), 96.

21. Bono and Assayas, *Bono*, 186.

22. Cited in Steve Stockman, *Walk On: The Spiritual Journey of U2* (Orlando, FL: Relevant Books, 2005), 59.

23. "Out on His Own," in Stokes, *U2: Three Chords and the Truth*, 62.

24. Niall Stokes, *U2: The Stories behind Every U2 Song* (London: Carlton, 2009), 50.

25. Christian Scharen, *One Step Closer: Why U2 Matters to Those Seeking God* (Grand Rapids, MI: Brazos Press, 2006), 153.

26. Cited in Alan, *U2: Wide Awake in America*, 84.

27. "All Ireland Champions!," in Stokes, *The U2 File*, 150.

28. Jackson, *Bono*, 42.

29. Cited in Waters, *Race of Angels*, 200.

30. Harry Browne, *The Frontman: Bono (In the Name of Power)* (London: Verso, 2013), 59.

31. Both cited in U2 and Neil McCormick, *U2 by U2* (New York: HarperCollins, 2006), 158.

32. Block, "Pure Bono (Part 1)."

33. U2 and McCormick, *U2 by U2*, 162.

34. U2 and McCormick, *U2 by U2*, 164; Stockman, *Walk On*, 44.

35. Matt McGee, *U2: A Diary* (London: Omnibus, 2008), 95.

36. "The Great Leap of Faith," in Stokes, *U2: Three Chords and the Truth*, 40.

37. Bono and Assayas, *Bono*, 238.

38. Louise Davis, "Feeding the World a Line? Celebrity Activism and Ethical Consumer Practices from Live Aid to Product Red," *Nordic Journal of English Studies* 9, no. 3 (2010): 89–117.

39. Wenner, "Bono," 58. The trip was so low-key that it did not even figure in Eamon Dunphy's 1987 band biography. Proceeds from the display in Hendricks Gallery in Dublin went to World Vision and Concern. The photographs were eventually published in Bono, *A String of Pearls: Photographs of Ethiopia* (N.p.: 1988) and in Bono, *On the Move: A Speech* (Nashville, TN: W. Publishing Group, 2007).

40. Cited in *U2: The Ultimate Compendium*, 65.

41. Alan, *U2 Wide Awake in America*, 247.

42. Cited in *U2: The Ultimate Compendium*, 65.

43. Cited in Dave Bowler and Bryan Dray, *U2: A Conspiracy of Hope* (London: Sidgwick & Jackson, 1993), 195.

44. U2 and McCormick, *U2 by U2*, 167, 169.

45. Cited in Alan, *U2: Wide Awake in America*, 245. See also U2 and McCormick, *U2 by U2*, 169.

46. Cited in Alan, *U2: Wide Awake in America*, 11.

47. *The Charlie Rose Show*, May 16, 2013, www.atu2.com/news/video-bonos-interview-with-charlie-rose.html, accessed November 11, 2014.

48. "The Homecoming" and "Stories of Boys," in Stokes, *The U2 File*, 141, 146.

49. Alan, *U2: Wide Awake in America*, 239.

50. Jackson, *Bono*, 171.

51. Alan, *U2: Wide Awake in America*, 239.

52. Cited in "Out on His Own," 61. See the performance at www.youtube.com/watch?v=cNASMkj0Dyc, accessed November 11, 2014.

53. Martha P. Trachtenberg, *Bono: Rock Star Activist* (Berkeley Heights, NJ: Enslow Publishers, 2008), 45; Višnja Cogan, *U2: An Irish Phenomenon* (Cork: The Collins Press, 2006), 129.

54. Browne, *The Frontman*, 25–26.

55. Cited in "Out on His Own," 61.

56. Cited in *U2: The Ultimate Compendium*, 53, 52.

57. Cited in McGee, *U2*, 81.

58. Healey cited in *U2: The Ultimate Compendium*, 46; see also Bowler and Dray, *U2*, 98.

59. McGee, *U2*, 88.

60. *U2: The Ultimate Compendium*, 49.

61. Pete Singer, cited in "Wide Awake in America," in Stokes, *U2: Three Chords and the Truth*, 50.

62. U2 and McCormick, *U2 by U2*, 174.

63. Henke, "The Edge."

64. Clayton, cited in Geoff Parkyn, *U2: Touch the Flame* (New York: Perigree Books, 1988), 74.

65. Bono, *Bono*, 26.

66. Dunphy, *Unforgettable Fire*, 266.

67. Bono, cited in U2 and McCormick, *U2 by U2*, 169.

68. McGee, *U2*, 97–98; Bono, *Bono*, 91; Bono and Assayas, *Bono*, 197–209; another group responsible for their travel was Sanctuary and David Batstone, Wendy Brown, and Howard Hoyle, all from the San Francisco Bay Area.

69. Cited in *U2: The Ultimate Compendium*, 96.

70. "The World about Us," 77; Bono, *Bono*, 92.

71. *U2: The Best of Propaganda: 20 Years of the Official U2 Magazine* (New York: Thunder's Mouth Press, 2003), 63.

72. U2 and McCormick, *U2 by U2*, 177.

73. Cited in *U2: The Ultimate Compendium*, 96.

74. Bono and Assayas, *Bono*, 198.

75. Cited in *U2: The Ultimate Compendium*, 96.

76. Browne, *The Frontman*, 124–26.

77. Bono and Assayas, *Bono*, 196, 198.

78. Bill Flanagan, *U2 at the End of the World* (New York: Dell, 1995), 346.

79. U2 and McCormick, *U2 by U2*, 179.

80. *U2: The Ultimate Compendium*, xx.

81. Jeff Malpas, "Philosophizing Place in *The Joshua Tree*," in Wrathall, *U2 and Philosophy*, 43, 50.

82. Cited in *U2: The Ultimate Compendium*, 69, 70, 99.

83. "The World about Us," 77, 78.

84. "A Mighty Long Way Down Rock 'n' Roll," in Stokes, *U2: Three Chords and the Truth*, 128.

85. "The World about Us," 79.

86. Bono and Assayas, *Bono*, 135.

87. Bono later confessed that U2 probably should have canceled; see Brian Libby, "Bono," reproduced in *The U2 Reader: A Quarter Century of Commentary, Criticism, and Reviews*, ed. Hank Bordowitz (Milwaukee, WI: Hal Leonard, 2003), 157.

88. Jackson, *Bono's Politics*, 35–36; *U2: The Ultimate Compendium*, 71; U2 and McCormick, *U2 by U2*, 197; McGee, *U2*, 102.

89. Bono and Assayas, *Bono*, 307.

90. McGee, *U2*, 66; Jackson, *Bono*, 102.

91. Block, "Pure Bono (Part 1)."

92. *U2: The Ultimate Compendium*, 60.

93. John Waters, "Deus ex Machina: The Band Who Grew to Earth," in Dunphy, *Unforgettable Fire*, 309–10.

3. ZOOROPA, 1990–1998

1. Mick Wall, *Bono: In the Name of Love* (New York: Thunder's Mouth Press, 2005), 183.

2. "A Mighty Long Way Down Rock 'n' Roll," in *U2: Three Chords and the Truth*, ed. Niall Stokes (New York: Harmony Books, 1989), 126–27.

3. Bono, cited in John Waters, *Race of Angels: The Genesis of U2* (London: Fourth Estate, 1994), 206.

4. Mike Savage, Gaynor Bagnall, and Brian Longhurst, *Globalization and Belonging* (London: Sage, 2005), 3.

5. Bill Flanagan, *U2 at the End of the World* (New York: Dell, 1995), 1.

6. Robert Vagacs, *Religious Nuts, Political Fanatics: U2 in Theological Perspective* (Eugene, OR: Cascade Books, 2005), 50.

7. Kerry Soper, "The Importance of Being Bono: The Philosophy and Politics of Identity in the Lyrics and Personae of U2's Frontman," in *U2 and Philosophy: How to Decipher an Atomic Band*, ed. Mark A. Wrathall (Chicago: Open Court, 2006), 71.

8. Scott Calhoun, "Introduction," in *Exploring U2: Is This Rock 'n' Roll? Essays on the Music, Work, and Influence of U2*, ed. Scott Calhoun (Lanham, MD: Scarecrow Press, 2012), xxv.

9. Waters, *Race of Angels*, 293.

10. John Hutchinson, "Luminous Times: U2 Wrestle with Their Moment of Glory," reproduced in *The U2 Reader: A Quarter Century of Commentary, Criticism, and Reviews*, ed. Hank Bordowitz (Milwaukee, WI: Hal Leonard, 2003), 61.

11. Elizabeth Wurtzel, "Me2," reproduced in Bordowitz, *The U2 Reader*, 93.

12. James Henke, "The Edge: The Rolling Stone Interview," *Rolling Stone*, March 10, 1987, www.atu2.com/news/the-edge-the-rolling-stone-interview.html.

13. Flanagan, *U2 at the End of the World*, 5.

14. Bobby Maddex, "A God-Shaped Hole: Can U2 and a New Generations of Seekers Ever Fill It?," *Gadfly*, August 1997, n.p.

15. Flanagan, *U2 at the End of the World*, 7.

16. Cited in Waters, *Race of Angels*, 206.

17. Matt McGee, *U2: A Diary* (London: Omnibus, 2008), 129.

18. For scholarly analyses of these performances, see Hubert L. Dreyfus and Mark A. Wrathall, "Staring at the Sun: U2 and the Experience of Kierkegaardian Despair," in Wrathall, *U2 and Philosophy*, 15–24; Susan Fast, "Music, Contexts, and Meaning in U2," in *Expression in Pop-Rock Music*, ed. Walter Everett (New York: Routledge, 2000), 33–57; Stephen Catanzarite, *Achtung Baby: Meditations on Love in the Shadow of the Fall* (New York: Continuum, 2007); Kevin J. H. Dettmar, "Nothing Succeeds Like Failure: U2 and the Politics of Irony," and Deane Galbraith, "Fallen Angels in the Hands of U2," in Calhoun, *Exploring U2*, 112–28, 179–96; and Robyn Brothers, "Time to Heal, 'Desire' Time: The Cyberprophesy of U2's 'Zoo World Tour,'" in *Reading Rock and Roll: Authenticity, Appropriation, Aesthetics*, ed. Kevin J. H. Dettmar and William Richey (New York: Columbia University Press, 1999), 237–67.

19. McGee, *U2*, 143.

20. Cited in Laura Jackson, *Bono: His Life, Music, and Passions* (New York: Citadel Press, 2003), 117.

21. Bono and Michka Assayas, *Bono* (New York: Riverhead Books, 2005), 297, 106.

22. B. P. Fallon, *U2 Faraway So Close* (Boston: Little, Brown, 1994), n.p.

23. Cited in Waters, *Race of Angels*, 298.

24. Cited in Christian Scharen, *One Step Closer: Why U2 Matters to Those Seeking God* (Grand Rapids, MI: Brazos Press, 2006), 66–67.

25. Waters, *Race of Angels*, 7, 13; Flanagan, *U2 at the End of the World*, 13.

26. Cited in Jackson, *Bono*, 150.

27. Cited in Flanagan, *U2 at the End of the World*, 71.

28. Cited in Flanagan, *U2 at the End of the World*, 68–70.

29. Cited in Nathan Dwayne Jackson, *Bono's Politics: The Future of Celebrity Political Activism* (Saarbrücken: VDM Verlag Dr. Müller, 2008), 40, and in Višnja Cogan, *U2: An Irish Phenomenon* (Cork: The Collins Press, 2006), 129.

30. "Sue," cited in Jackson, *Bono*, 123.

31. *U2: The Best of Propaganda: 20 Years of the Official U2 Magazine* (New York: Thunder's Mouth Press, 2003), 169.

32. All cited in Flanagan, *U2 at the End of the World*, 97, 167, 172.

33. Cited in *U2: The Best of Propaganda*, 174.

34. Tassoula E. Kokkoris, "Secrets of Sarajevo: 20 Years Later," *@U2*, April 26, 2013, www.atu2.com/news/secrets-of-sarajevo-20-years-later.html, accessed November 11, 2014.

35. Cited in Flanagan, *U2 at the End of the World*, 277, 285.

36. Both cited in Flanagan, *U2 at the End of the World*, 295, 294, 299.

37. Cited in *U2: The Best of Propaganda*, 174.

38. Cited in Flanagan, *U2 at the End of the World*, 307.

39. Cited in Waters, *Race of Angels*, 21.

40. Cited in *U2: The Best of Propaganda*, 175, 176.

41. Kokkoris, "Secrets of Sarajevo."

42. Cited in Harry Browne, *The Frontman: Bono (In the Name of Power)* (London: Verso, 2013), 128.

43. Cited in Flanagan, *U2 at the End of the World*, 309.

44. Both cited in *U2: The Ultimate Compendium of Interviews, Articles, Facts, and Opinions from the Files of* Rolling Stone (New York: Hyperion, 1994), 208.

45. Flanagan, *U2 at the End of the World*, 307.

46. Kokkoris, "Secrets of Sarajevo." See also Aida Cerkez and Sabina Niksic, "1993 Bosnian Beauty Queen Stood Up against War," Associated Press, April 4, 2012, http://cnsnews.com/news/article/1993-bosnian-beauty-queen-stood-against-war, accessed November 25, 2014.

47. Jackson, *Bono*, 151.

48. U2 and Neil McCormick, *U2 by U2* (New York: HarperCollins, 2006), 277–79; Jackson, *Bono's Politics*, 50.

49. McGee, *U2*, 135, 159, 166.

50. Wall, *Bono*, 184.

51. McGee, *U2*, 160, 181.

52. Jackson, *Bono*, 159.

53. McGee, *U2*, 184.

54. Jackson, *Bono*, 174.

55. Jackson, *Bono*, 176.

56. Bono and Assayas, *Bono*, 192.

57. Browne, *The Frontman*, 35.

58. Fachtna O'Ceallaigh, cited in Dermott Hayes, "Do You Know This Man?," reproduced in Bordowitz, *The U2 Reader*, 253.

59. Wall, *Bono*, 210.

60. Cited in U2 and McCormick, *U2 by U2*, 286.

4. BONO, SUPERSTAR LOBBYIST, 1999–2005

1. Cited in Josh Tyrangiel, "Music: Bono," *Time*, March 4, 2002, www.time.com/time/magazine/article/0,9171,1001931-1,00.html.

2. Cited in *U2: The Ultimate Compendium of Interviews, Articles, Facts, and Opinions from the Files of* Rolling Stone (New York: Hyperion, 1994), 120.

3. Bono and Michka Assayas, *Bono* (New York: Riverhead Books, 2005), 46.

4. Cited in "Bono: 'I'm Tired of Just Dreaming,'" *Irish Independent*, March 2, 2002, www.atu2.com/news/bono-im-tired-of-just-dreaming.html, accessed April 18, 2014.

5. See, for example, Paul Collier, *The Bottom Billion: Why the Poorest Countries Are Failing and What Can Be Done about It* (New York: Oxford University Press, 2007).

6. Cited in Bono and Assayas, *Bono*, 260.

7. Varihi Scott, "Big Dog Celebrity Activists: Barking up the Wrong Tree," in *Transnational Celebrity Activism in Global Politics: Changing the World?*, ed. Liza Tsaliki, Christos A. Frangonikolopoulos, and Asteris Huliaras (Chicago: Intellect, 2011), 284.

8. Asteris Huliaras and Nikolaos Tzifakis, "Bringing the Individuals Back In? Celebrities as Transnational Activists," in Tsaliki et al., *Transnational Celebrity Activism*, 31.

9. Cited in Bono and Assayas, *Bono*, 90.

10. Bono and Assayas, *Bono*, 211, 137.

11. www.looktothestars.org, accessed February 9, 2015.

12. "Introduction," in *Global Development 2.0: Can Philanthropists, the Public, and the Poor Make Poverty History?*, ed. Lael Brainard and Derek Chollet (Washington, DC: Brookings Institution Press, 2008), 3.

13. Dan Brockington, *Celebrity Advocacy and International Development* (New York: Routledge, 2014), 21, 25.

14. Lael Brainard and Vinca LaFleur, "Making Poverty History? How Activists, Philanthropists, and the Public Are Changing Global Development," in Brainard and Chollet, *Global Development 2.0*, 9–12; Matthew Bishop, "Fighting Global Poverty: Who Will Be Relevant in 2020?," in Brainard and Chollet, *Global Development 2.0*, 46.

15. Portman and Bono, cited in James Traub, "The Celebrity Solution," *New York Times*, March 9, 2008.

16. Brockington, *Celebrity Advocacy and International Development*, 41.

17. Huliaras and Tzifakis, "Bringing the Individuals Back In?," 37.

18. Matt McGee, *U2: A Diary* (London: Omnibus, 2008), 214; Huliaras and Tzifakis, "Bringing the Individuals Back In?," 32.

19. Dorothy Njoroge, "Calling a New Tune for Africa? Analysing a Celebrity-Led Campaign to Redefine the Debate on Africa," in Tsaliki et al., *Transnational Celebrity Activism*, 235.

20. Ulf Hannerz, "Cosmopolitans and Locals in World Culture," *Theory, Culture and Society* 7 (1990): 237–51; Annika Bergman Rosamond, "The Cosmopolitan-Communitarian Divide and Celebrity Anti-War Activism," in Tsaliki et al., *Transnational Celebrity Activism*, 67.

21. Cited in Riina Yrjölä, "The Global Politics of Celebrity Humanitarianism," in Tsaliki et al., 177.

22. Liza Tsaliki, Christos A. Frangonikolopoulos, and Asteris Huliaras, "Conclusion: Making Sense of Transnational Celebrity Activism: Causes, Methods and Consequences," in *Transnational Celebrity Activism*, 299.

23. Mark Malloch Brown, cited in David Rothkopf, *Superclass: The Global Power Elite and the World They Are Making* (New York: Farrar, Straus and Giroux, 2008), 236.

24. Greg Garrett, *We Get to Carry Each Other: The Gospel According to U2* (Louisville, KY: Westminster John Knox Press, 2009), 112.

25. *The Charlie Rose Show*, May 16, 2013, www.atu2.com/news/video-bonos-interview-with-charlie-rose.html, accessed November 11, 2014.

26. Višnja Cogan, *U2: An Irish Phenomenon* (Cork: The Collins Press, 2006), 51.

27. Bono speech at the European People's Party summit, Dublin, March 7, 2014, www.youtube.com/watch?v=2fHcxwwt-LQ, accessed September 18, 2014.

28. Bono, "Transcript of Bono's Class Day Speech at Harvard," June 10, 2001, reproduced in *The U2 Reader: A Quarter Century of Commentary, Criticism, and Reviews*, ed. Hank Bordowitz (Milwaukee, WI: Hal Leonard, 2003), 153. See also Noreena Hertz, *The Debt Threat: How Debt Is Destroying the Developing World* (New York: HarperCollins, 2004).

29. *U2: The Best of Propaganda: 20 Years of the Official U2 Magazine* (New York: Thunder's Mouth Press, 2003), 264; Brian Libby, "Bono," reproduced in Bordowitz, *The U2 Reader*, 160.

30. "Can Bono Save the Third World?," *The Daily Beast*, January 23, 2000, www.thedailybeast.com/newsweek/2000/01/23/can-bono-save-the-third-world.html, accessed November 11, 2014.

31. Nathan Dwayne Jackson, *Bono's Politics: The Future of Celebrity Political Activism* (Saarbrücken: VDM Verlag Dr. Müller, 2008), 65–69; Hertz, *The Debt Threat*, 4.

32. Martha P. Trachtenberg, *Bono: Rock Star Activist* (Berkeley Heights, NJ: Enslow Publishers, 2008), 74.

33. "Can Bono Save the Third World?"

34. Alan Light, "Band of the Year: Rock's Unbreakable Heart," *Spin*, January 1, 2002, www.atu2.com/news/band-of-the-year-rocks-unbreakable-heart.html, accessed November 11, 2014.

35. "Stars Condemn G8 Violence," BBC News, July 22, 2001, http://news.bbc.co.uk/2/hi/entertainment/1451528.stm, accessed April 11, 2014.

36. He appeared alone in the March 4, 2003, issue; with other celebrities in *Time Europe*'s celebration of "European Heroes" in the April 28, 2003, issue; in a collage for the "*Time* 100" in the April 16, 2004, issue; and with the Gateses in the December 26, 2005–January 2, 2006, issue. He appeared a few other times on the cover but unrelated to his activism.

37. Cited in Jackson, *Bono's Politics*, 77.

38. Trachtenberg, *Bono*, 74–80; Jackson, *Bono's Politics*, 78.

39. Anthony DeCurtis, "Bono's Crusade," *Rolling Stone*, March 6, 2002, www.atu2.com/news/bonos-crusade-1.html, accessed November 11, 2014.

40. Bono letter to George W. Bush, Killiney, December 29, 2004, www.georgewbushlibrary.smu.edu/~/media/GWBL/Images/Galleries/Sneak-Peek-Document/BonoLetter_Page_1.ashx, accessed October 2, 2014.

41. Jackson, *Bono's Politics*, 69; Hertz, *The Debt Threat*, 4.

42. Tyrangiel, "Music"; Joshua Busby, "Is There a Constituency for Global Poverty? Jubilee 2000 and the Future of Development Advocacy," in Brainard and Chollet, *Global Development 2.0*, 90; Hertz, *The Debt Threat*, 13.

43. Cited in McGee, *U2*, 222.

44. Bono and Assayas, *Bono*, 99.

45. Cited in Bono and Assayas, *Bono*, 165.

46. Cited in U2 and Neil McCormick, *U2 by U2* (New York: HarperCollins, 2006), 290.

47. Cited in "Bono's World," reproduced in Bordowitz, *The U2 Reader*, 141, and in DeCurtis, "Bono's Crusade."

48. Busby, "Is There a Constituency for Global Poverty?," 95.

49. Jonathan Curiel, "Star Power: When Celebrities Support Causes, Who Really Winds Up Benefiting?," *SF Gate*, June 5, 2005, www.sfgate.com/opinion/article/Star-power-When-celebrities-support-causes-who-2665234.php, accessed April 17, 2014.

50. Cited in Stephen McGinty, "Bono Still Hasn't Found What He Is Looking For: Debt Relief," *The Scotsman*, September 25, 2004, www.atu2.com/news/bono-still-hasnt-found-what-he-is-looking-for-debt-relief.html, accessed November 11, 2014.

51. Stephanie Flanders, Sheryl Sandberg, and Larry Summers, cited in Hertz, *The Debt Threat*, 9, 10.

52. Cited in U2 and McCormick, *U2 by U2*, 290.

53. Cited in Andrew Essex, "Unforgettable Fire: The Ongoing Beatification of Bono," *U2-Atomic-Articles*, October 22, 2001, http://u2-atomic-articles.tripod.com/id73.html, accessed November 11, 2014.

54. Cited in Garrett, *We Get to Carry Each Other*, 114.

55. Busby, "Is There a Constituency for Global Poverty?," 88.

56. Harry Browne, *The Frontman: Bono (In the Name of Power)* (London: Verso, 2013), 70, 75; Hertz, *The Debt Threat*, 11.

57. Joshua William Busby, "Bono Made Jesse Helms Cry: Jubilee 2000, Debt Relief, and Moral Action in International Politics," *International Studies Quarterly* 51 (June 2007): 248.

58. Cited in Busby, "Is There a Constituency for Global Poverty?," 86.

59. Erik Philbrook, "Keeping the Peace," reproduced in Bordowitz, *The U2 Reader*, 130.

60. Libby, "Bono," 159.

61. Philbrook, "Keeping the Peace," 133.

62. Bono, "University of Pennsylvania Commencement," May 17, 2004, www.c-span.org/video/?181946-1/university-pennsylvania-commencement, accessed November 11, 2014.

63. Cited in Robert Vagacs, *Religious Nuts, Political Fanatics: U2 in Theological Perspective* (Eugene, OR: Cascade Books, 2005), 65.

64. Bono and Assayas, *Bono*, 218.

65. Arthur E. Lizie, *Dreaming the World: U2 Fans, Online Community and Intellectual Communication* (Cresskill, NJ: Hampton Press, 2009), ix. See also Niall Stokes, *U2: The Stories behind Every U2 Song* (London: Carlton, 2009), 156.

66. Jackson, *Bono's Politics*, 17, 153.

67. Cited in Eamon Javers, "Bono's K Street Connection," *CQ Weekly*, March 28, 2005, 762–63.

68. Traub, "The Celebrity Solution."

69. U2 and McCormick, *U2 by U2*, 314.

70. Steve Stockman, *Walk On: The Spiritual Journey of U2* (Orlando, FL: Relevant Books, 2005), 195.

71. Bono and Assayas, *Bono*, 137.

72. Bono and Assayas, *Bono*, 92.

73. Bono and Assayas, *Bono*, 90.

74. Cited in Mick Wall, *Bono: In the Name of Love* (New York: Thunder's Mouth Press, 2005), 251.

75. Bono and Assayas, *Bono*, 257.

76. Cited in DeCurtis, "Bono's Crusade."

77. William W. Fisher III and Cyrill P. Rigamonti, "The South African AIDS Controversy: A Case Study in Patent Law and Policy," Harvard Law School, February 2005, http://cyber.law.harvard.edu/people/tfisher/South%20Africa.pdf, accessed February 21, 2014, 2–7, 23, 27.

78. Cathleen Falsani, "Bono's American Prayer," *Christianity Today*, March 1, 2003, www.christianitytoday.com/ct/2003/marchweb-only/2.38.html, accessed November 11, 2014.

79. U2 and McCormick, *U2 by U2*, 339.

80. Cited in McGinty, "Bono Still Hasn't Found What He Is Looking For."

81. Cited in Browne, *The Frontman*, 74.

82. Anthony DeCurtis, "Bono: The Beliefnet Interview," February 2001, www.beliefnet.com/Entertainment/Music/2001/02/Bono-The-Beliefnet-Interview.aspx, accessed November 11, 2014.

83. Tyrangiel, "Music"; Jackson, *Bono's Politics*, 97.

84. Trachtenberg, *Bono*, 93.

85. Bono and Assayas, *Bono*, 292.

86. Niall Stokes, "Matter of Life and Death—Part 1," *Hot Press Annual 2002*, December 1, 2001, www.atu2.com/news/matter-of-life-and-death-part-1.html, accessed November 11, 2014.

87. Bono to Bush, December 29, 2004.

88. Cited in James Traub, "The Statesman," *New York Times Magazine*, September 18, 2005, www.nytimes.com/2005/09/18/magazine/18bono.html?pagewanted=print, accessed April 4, 2014.

89. "Bono: Not Facing AIDS Crisis 'Foolhardy,'" Fox News, September 1, 2004, www.foxnews.com/story/2004/09/02/bono-not-facing-aids-crisis-foolhardy, accessed November 11, 2014.

90. Ann-Louis Colgan, "Africa Policy Outlook 2005," *Foreign Policy in Focus*, October 3, 2005, http://fpif.org/africa_policy_outlook_2005, accessed April 4, 2014; Bono to Bush, December 29, 2004.

91. Bono, cited in Brian Hiatt, "Trying to Throw Their Arms around the World," *Rolling Stone*, November 6, 2014, 57; Chad E. Seales, "Burned over Bono: U2's Rock 'n' Roll Messiah and His Religious Politic," *Journal of Religion and Popular Culture* 14, no. 1 (2006): n.p.

92. Stephen Catanzarite, "All That We Can't Leave Behind: U2's Conservative Voice," in *Exploring U2: Is This Rock 'n' Roll? Essays on the Music, Work, and Influence of U2*, ed. Scott Calhoun (Lanham, MD: Scarecrow Press, 2012), 229–39.

93. Bono to Bush, December 29, 2004.

94. Jann S. Wenner, "Bono: The Rolling Stone Interview," *Rolling Stone*, November 3, 2005, 56; Angela Pancella, "The Nashville Summit: Behind the Scenes with Bono, Data and the Christian Music Industry," July 28, 2003, www.atu2.com/news/the-nashville-summit-behind-the-scenes-with-bono-data-and-the-christian-music-industry.html, accessed November 11, 2014.

95. Cited in Jackson, *Bono's Politics*, 220.

96. Bono, cited in Wenner, "Bono," 56.

97. Busby, "Bono Made Jesse Helms Cry," 248, 268.

98. Bono and Assayas, *Bono*, 199–200.

99. Bono, "Transcript of Video Message Recorded for Christian Music Festivals, plus Extrapolations," in *The aWAKE Project: United against the African AIDS Crisis*, ed. Jenny Eaton and Kate Etue (Nashville, TN: W. Publishing Group, 2002), 80–82.

100. Pancella, "The Nashville Summit." See also Bono, *On the Move: A Speech* (Nashville, TN: W Publishing Group, 2007).

101. Christian Scharen, *One Step Closer: Why U2 Matters to Those Seeking God* (Grand Rapids, MI: Brazos Press, 2006), 187. See also Falsani, "Bono's American Prayer."

102. Cited in McGee, *U2*, 252.

103. Cited in Falsani, "Bono's American Prayer."

104. "Bono's Thin Ecclesiology," *Christianity Today*, March 1, 2003, www.christianitytoday.com/ct/2003/marchweb-only/29.37.html, accessed April 7, 2014.

105. Cited in Stockman, *Walk On*, 207–10.

106. Falsani, "Bono's American Prayer."

107. Garrett, *We Get to Carry Each Other*, 15.

108. Tom Zeller Jr., "Bono, Trying to Throw His Arms around the World," *New York Times*, November 13, 2006. See also Beth Maynard, "Where *Leitourgia* Has No Name: U2 Live," in Calhoun, *Exploring U2*, 151–64.

109. Cited in Bobby Maddex, "A God-Shaped Hole: Can U2 and a New Generation of Seekers Ever Fill It?," *Gadfly*, August 1997, n.p.

110. Seales, "Burned over Bono," n.p.

111. Raewynne J. Whiteley and Beth Maynard, eds., *Get Up Off Your Knees: Preaching the U2 Catalog* (Cambridge, MA: Cowley Publications, 2003), 10, 12.

112. Hertz, *The Debt Threat*, 14.

113. Busby, "Bono Made Jesse Helms Cry," 268–69.

114. Hertz, *The Debt Threat*, 18, 16–17.

115. Bono, *On the Move*, 20.

116. Jeffrey D. Sachs, *The End of Poverty: Economic Possibilities for Our Time* (New York: Penguin, 2005), 344.

117. Editorial, *Washington Post*, July 14, 2004, A18.

118. Jackson, *Bono's Politics*, 187.

119. Trachtenberg, *Bono*, 104.

120. http://en.wikipedia.org/wiki/The_Girl_in_the_Café, accessed February 20, 2014.

121. Jackson, *Bono's Politics*, 185.

122. Cited in Homi Kharas, "The New Reality of Aid," in Brainard and Chollet, *Global Development 2.0*, 53.

123. Cited in Cogan, *U2*, 147.

124. Cited in Jackson, *Bono's Politics*, 188.

125. Cited in Rothkopf, *Superclass*, 235.

126. Cited in Brockington, *Celebrity Advocacy and International Development*, 7.

127. Cited in Wall, *Bono*, 259.

5. CONSOLIDATION AND CRITICISM, 2006–2015

1. Bono, *Bono: In His Own Words* (New York: Omnibus Press, 1997), 73.

2. "U2 Tops Billboard's Money Makers Chart," *Billboard*, n.d., www.billboard.com/articles/news/59982/u2-tops-billboards-money-makers-chart, accessed April 4, 2014.

3. http://en.wikipedia.org/wiki/List_of_highest-grossing_concert_tours, accessed November 11, 2014.

4. Rob Sheffield, review of "Music from 'Spider-Man: Turn Off the Dark,'" *Rolling Stone*, June 14, 2011, www.rollingstone.com/music/albumreviews/music-from-spider-man-turn-off-the-dark-20110614, accessed April 4, 2014.

5. Bono, "Message 2U," *Vanity Fair*, July 2007, 32.

6. Examples include the 2003 MusiCares Person of the Year Award from the Recording Academy; the Chevalier of Legion of Honor from France; a Humanitarian Award from the American Ireland Fund National Gala; Honorary Citizenship from Turin, Italy; the 2004 Freedom Award at the National Civil Rights Museum in Memphis, Tennessee; the 2005 Ambassador of Conscience Award for the band as a whole from Amnesty International; the German Media Award; the Pablo Neruda Merit Award from Chile; a knighthood from the Queen of England but without the honorific "sir" reserved for British citizens; and the National Association for the Advancement of Colored People's Chairman Award.

7. Cited in Bono and Michka Assayas, *Bono* (New York: Riverhead Books, 2005), 265, and Laura Jackson, *Bono: His Life, Music, and Passions* (New York: Citadel Press, 2003), 166.

8. http://musicrising.org/about, accessed April 11, 2014; "It's All about the Vision," *The Independent*, May 16, 2006, Extra section, 14; "Music Rising at Tulane Launches Musical Cultures Innovative Learning Platform," April 17, 2014, http://musicrising.org/posts/1911/music-rising-at-tulane-launches-musical-cultures-innovative-learning-platform, accessed April 25, 2014.

9. Melena Ryzik, "Charlize Theron's Influence, Anderson Cooper's Help," *New York Times*, January 12, 2014, http://carpetbagger.blogs.nytimes.com/2014/01/12/charlize-therons-influence-anderson-coopers-help, accessed April 14, 2014.

10. Martha P. Trachtenberg, *Bono: Rock Star Activist* (Berkeley Heights, NJ: Enslow Publishers, 2008); U2 and Neil McCormick, *U2 by U2* (New York: HarperCollins, 2006), 295; Jackson, *Bono*, 208. See also Michael Gilmour, "The Prophet Jeremiah, Aung San Suu Kyi, and U2's *All That You Can't Leave Behind*: On Listening to Bono's Jeremiad," in *Call Me the Seeker: Listening to Religion in Popular Music*, ed. Michael Gilmour (New York: Continuum, 2005), 34–43.

11. Cited in "Electric Burma for Aung San Suu Kyi," June 18, 2012, www.u2.com/news/article/6356.

12. Elysa Gardner, "Bono's Looking Back, and Ahead, and Within," *USA Today*, January 31, 2014, 7B.

13. "U2 Speak of Their 'Long History' with Mandela," *RTÉ*, November 26, 2013, www.rte.ie/ten/news/2013/1126/489237-u2-speak-of-their-long-history-with-mandela, accessed April 14, 2014.

14. "U2 Minus 1-Live in New York Tonight," www.u2.com/news/title/u2-minus-1-live-in-new-york-tonight, accessed December 2, 2014. The entire concert is also here.

15. Jeff Zeleny, "The 2008 Campaign: Bono's Poverty-Fighting Plan Promoted by Two Ex-Senators," *New York Times*, June 12, 2007.

16. Bono, "Message 2U," 32.

17. www.one.org/us/about, accessed February 9, 2015, cited in Randall Lane, "Bill Gates and Bono: 'Partners in Crime' Discuss Their Collaboration for Good [Video]," *Forbes*, June 6, 2013, www.forbes.com/sites/randalllane/2013/06/06/bill-gates-and-bono-on-ending-global-poverty, accessed April 4, 2014; Bono, "M.D.G.'s for Beginners . . . and Finishers," *New York Times*, September 18, 2010, www.nytimes.com/2010/09/19/opinion/19bono.html?pagewanted=all, accessed April 11, 2014. For more on transparency, see the webcast "U2's Bono Speaks at GU Global Social Enterprise Event," November 12, 2012, www.georgetown.edu/webcast/bono-social-enterprise.html, accessed April 11, 2014.

18. David Heim, "Breakfast with Bono," *Christian Century*, March 21, 2006, 21.

19. Cited in Greg Garrett, *We Get to Carry Each Other: The Gospel According to U2* (Louisville, KY: Westminster John Knox Press, 2009), 104.

20. Cited in Greg Kot, "Bono: 'We Need to Talk,'" *Chicago Tribune*, May 22, 2005, http://articles.chicagotribune.com/2005-05-22/news/0505220011_1_achtung-baby-band-adam-clayton/4, accessed April 4, 2014.

21. David Carr, "Citizen Bono Brings Africa to the Idle Rich," *New York Times*, March 5, 2007, www.nytimes.com/2007/03/05/business/media/05carr.html?_r=0, accessed April 11, 2014; "Bono and Bob Geldof to Guest-Edit the Globe and Mail," May 5, 2010, www.one.org/us/2010/05/05/bono-and-bob-geldof-to-guest-edit-the-globe-and-mail, accessed April 15, 2014; "Bono to Edit Newspaper for a Day," May 5, 2006, BBC News, http://news.bbc.co.uk/2/hi/entertainment/4976406.stm, accessed April 15, 2014; Matt McGee, *U2: A Diary* (London: Omnibus, 2008), 324.

22. Nathan Dwayne Jackson, *Bono's Politics: The Future of Celebrity Political Activism* (Saarbrücken: VDM Verlag Dr. Müller, 2008), 168.

23. www.one.org/us/about, accessed February 9, 2015. See also Bono speech at the European People's Party Summit, Dublin, March 7, 2014, www.youtube.com/watch?v=2fHcxwwt-LQ, accessed September 18, 2014; Chris O'Brien, "'Factivist' Bono Projects Poverty Rate of Zero by 2030," *Los Angeles Times*, February 26, 2013, www.latimes.com/business/technology/la-fi-tn-ted-2013-factivist-bono-projects-poverty-rate-of-zero-by-2030-20130226,0,173686.story, accessed April 4, 2014; *The Charlie Rose Show*, May 16, 2013, www.atu2.com/news/video-bonos-interview-with-charlie-rose.html, accessed April 4, 2014; Paul Bedard, "Bono: George Bush, Evangelicals Saved 9 Million AIDS Victims," *Washington Examiner*, June 24, 2013, http://washingtonexaminer.com/article/2532298, accessed April 11, 2014; and Bono, "M.D.G.'s for Beginners . . . and Finishers."

24. Lane, "Bill Gates and Bono."

25. Trachtenberg, *Bono*, 107.

26. Brian Hiatt, "Trying to Throw Their Arms around the World," *Rolling Stone*, November 6, 2014, 58; Stuart Elliott, "Product Red Steps Up Its Efforts with 'Lazarus Effect,'" *New York Times*, April 29, 2010. See the film at www.youtube.com/watch?v=ll6YH6xCN4c, accessed April 7, 2014.

27. Stefano Ponte, Lisa Ann Richey, and Mike Baab, "Bono's Product (RED) Initiative: Corporate Social Responsibility That Solves the Problems of 'Distant Others,'" *Third World Quarterly* 30, no. 2 (2009): 305–6.

28. "(RED), U2 and Bank of America Partner to Fight Aids," *PR Newswire*, January 23, 2014, www.prnewswire.com/news-releases/red-u2-and-bank-of-america-partner-to-fight-aids-241689131.html, accessed April 14, 2014.

29. Bono and Assayas, *Bono*, 315; John Masterson, "Ali's Other Eden," *Irish Independent*, March 8, 2005, www.atu2.com/news/alis-other-eden.html, accessed April 7, 2014.

30. Masterson, "Ali's Other Eden."

31. Nathalie Atkinson, "Ali Hewson and Bono's Return to Edun," *National Post*, March 5, 2011, http://arts.nationalpost.com/2011/03/05/ali-hewson-and-bonos-return-to-edun, accessed April 7, 2014; Elisabetta Povoledo, "For Fash-

ion's Glitterati, 'Trade Not Aid' Shoots through IHT Conference," *International Herald Tribune*, November 16, 2012; Suzy Menkes, "Philanthropy in Fashion," *New York Times*, November 15, 2012; Harry Browne, *The Frontman: Bono (In the Name of Power)* (London: Verso, 2013), 107–8; http://edun.com/about, accessed April 7, 2014.

32. Liza Tsaliki, Christos A. Frangonikolopoulos, and Asteris Huliaras, "Conclusion: Making Sense of Transnational Celebrity Activism: Causes, Methods and Consequences," in *Transnational Celebrity Activism in Global Politics: Changing the World?* (Chicago: Intellect, 2011), 305, 303.

33. Liza Tsaliki, Christos A. Frangonikolopoulos, and Asteris Huliaras, "Introduction: The Challenge of Transnational Celebrity Activism: Background, Aim and Scope of the Book," in *Transnational Celebrity Activism*, 11.

34. Lael Brainard and Vinca LaFleur, "Making Poverty History? How Activists, Philanthropists, and the Public Are Changing Global Development," in *Global Development 2.0: Can Philanthropists, the Public, and the Poor Make Poverty History?*, ed. Lael Brainard and Derek Chollet (Washington, DC: Brookings Institution Press, 2008), 22; Darrell M. West, "Angelina, Mia, and Bono: Celebrities and International Development," in Brainard and Chollet, *Global Development 2.0*, 75.

35. Tsaliki et al., "Introduction," 14; Louise Davis, "Feeding the World a Line? Celebrity Activism and Ethical Consumer Practices from Live Aid to Product Red," *Nordic Journal of English Studies* 9, no. 3 (2010): 89–117.

36. "A Look at the 50 Most Generous Donors of 2013," *The Chronicle of Philanthropy*, February 9, 2013, http://philanthropy.com/article/A-Look-at-the-50-Most-Generous/144529/#p50_list, accessed April 25, 2014. The absence of any celebrity was typical.

37. Niall Stokes, "U2—An Outstanding Artistic Force," *Hot Press*, October 30, 2014, www.hotpress.com/politics/themessage/U2---An-Outstanding-Artistic-Force/12817095.html?new_layout=1&page_no=1&show_comments=1, accessed November 7, 2014; Browne, *The Frontman*, 9.

38. James Traub, "The Celebrity Solution," *New York Times*, March 9, 2008.

39. Cited in Varihi Scott, "Big Dog Celebrity Activists: Barking Up the Wrong Tree," in Tsaliki et al., *Transnational Celebrity Activism*, 288.

40. Dan Brockington, *Celebrity Advocacy and International Development* (New York: Routledge, 2104), 8–9.

41. Richard Blow, "Bono Turns Up the Political Heat," *George Magazine*, April 1, 2000, www.atu2.com/news/bono-turns-up-the-political-heat.html, accessed November 11, 2014, cited in Bono and Assayas, *Bono*, 97; Browne, *The Frontman*, 145.

42. Bono, editorial, "I Am a Witness. What Can I Do?," *The Independent*, May 16, 2006, 38.

43. George Monbiot, "Bono Can't Help Africans by Stealing Their Voice," *The Guardian*, June 17, 2013, www.theguardian.com/commentisfree/2013/jun/17/bono-africans-stealing-voice-poor, accessed April 7, 2014; Riina Yrjölä, "The Global Politics of Celebrity Humanitarianism," in Tsaliki et al., *Transnational Celebrity Activism*, 186.

44. Fuse ODG, "Why I Had to Turn Down Band AID," *The Guardian*, November 19, 2014, www.theguardian.com/commentisfree/2014/nov/19/turn-down-band-aid-bob-geldof-africa-fuse-odg, accessed December 2, 2014; Carlos Chirinos, cited in "Band Aid 30 Faces Criticism for Being Damaging to Africa," BBC, November 18, 2014, www.bbc.co.uk/newsround/30097406, accessed November 18, 2014.

45. Browne, *The Frontman*, 159.

46. Browne, *The Frontman*, 79.

47. Cited in Mick Wall, *Bono: In the Name of Love* (New York: Thunder's Mouth Press, 2005), 253.

48. Browne, *The Frontman*, 4.

49. Scott, "Big Dog Celebrity Activists," 285; Browne, *The Frontman*, 83, cited in Traub, "The Celebrity Solution."

50. Cited in Bono and Assayas, *Bono*, 362.

51. Ponte et al., "Bono's Product (RED) Initiative," 302, 312, 313. See also Ron Nixon, "Bottom Line for (Red)," *New York Times*, February 6, 2008, www.nytimes.com/2008/02/06/business/06red.html?pagewanted=all, accessed April 7, 2014, cited in Tom Zeller Jr., "Bono, Trying to Throw His Arms around the World," *New York Times*, November 13, 2006, www.nytimes.com/2006/11/13/us/13bono.html?ref=jessehelms, accessed April 7, 2014.

52. Davis, "Feeding the World a Line?," 89–117.

53. Lisa Ann Richey and Stefano Ponte, *Brand Aid: Shopping Well to Save the World* (Minneapolis: University of Minnesota Press, 2011), xii, xiii–xiv.

54. Monbiot, "Bono Can't Help Africans by Stealing Their Voice"; Browne, *The Frontman*, 77, 153; Nick Cullather, *The Hungry World: America's Cold War Battle against Poverty in Asia* (Cambridge, MA: Harvard University Press, 2010), 261.

55. Cited in Ponte et al., "Bono's Product (RED) Initiative," 313; Bono, "I Am a Witness," 38; Lane, "Bill Gates and Bono"; Nixon, "Bottom Line for (Red)"; Barbara Kiviat and Bill Gates, "Making Capitalism More Creative," *Time*, July 31, 2008, www.time.com/time/magazine/article/0,9171,1828417-3,00.html, accessed April 4, 2014, cited in *The Charlie Rose Show*; Bono and Bruce Edwards, cited in Bruce Edwards, "Bono's Rhetoric of the Auspicious: Translating and Transforming Africa for the Consumerist West," in *Exploring U2: Is This Rock 'n' Roll? Essays on the Music, Work, and Influence of U2*, ed. Scott Calhoun (Lanham, MD: Scarecrow Press, 2012), 201.

56. See, for example, William Easterly's two books, *The Elusive Quest for Growth* (Cambridge, MA: MIT Press, 2001) and *The White Man's Burden* (New York: Penguin, 2007).

57. Niall Ferguson and Moyo, cited in Dambisa Moyo, *Dead Aid: Why Aid Is Not Working and How There Is a Better Way for Africa* (New York: Farrar, Straus and Giroux, 2009), x, 26; West, "Angelina, Mia, and Bono," 83, cited in Dorothy Njoroge, "Calling a New Tune for Africa? Analysing a Celebrity-Led Campaign to Redefine the Debate on Africa," in Tsaliki et al., *Transnational Celebrity Activism*, 242; Easterly, *The White Man's Burden*, 4–30.

58. Cullather, *The Hungry World*, 261.

59. Homi Kharas, "The New Reality of Aid," in Brainard and Chollet, *Global Development 2.0*, 55.

60. Cited in John Dart, "Bono: 'Juxtapositioning' for the World's Poor," *Christian Century*, February 13–20, 2002, 12.

61. Jackson, *Bono's Politics*, 102, 110.

62. Cited in McGee, *U2*, 248.

63. Bono and Assayas, *Bono*, 112.

64. Bono, "Africa Reboots," *New York Times*, April 17, 2010, www.nytimes.com/2010/04/18/opinion/18bono.html?pagewanted=all, accessed April 7, 2014.

65. *The Charlie Rose Show*.

66. Cited in Bono and Assayas, *Bono*, 114.

67. Cited in Bono and Assayas, *Bono*, 115, 289; Jeremy Laurence, "Why RED Can Boost Global Fund and Its War on HIV," *The Independent*, May 16, 2006, 2; Moyo, *Dead Aid*, xi.

68. Bono and Assayas, *Bono*, 111.

69. Browne, *The Frontman*, 76.

70. Stephen McGinty, "Bono Still Hasn't Found What He Is Looking For: Debt Relief," *The Scotsman*, September 25, 2004, www.atu2.com/news/bono-still-hasnt-found-what-he-is-looking-for-debt-relief.html, accessed November 11, 2014.

71. Bono letter to George W. Bush, Killiney, December 29, 2004, www.georgewbushlibrary.smu.edu/~/media/GWBL/Images/Galleries/Sneak-Peek-Document/BonoLetter_Page_1.ashx, accessed November 17, 2014.

72. Cited in Clifford Krauss, "Canada's Leader Is a Skinflint, Says a Former Admirer, Bono," *New York Times*, May 4, 2005; also in McGee, *U2*, 264.

73. Larry Elliott and David Teathe, "Blair Hails Push on Debt Relief for Poorest," *World Security Network*, June 11, 2004, www.worldsecuritynetwork.com/Other/Larry-Elliott-and-David-Teather-/Blair-hails-push-on-debt-relief-for-poorest, accessed April 4, 2014, cited in Bono and Assayas, *Bono*, 365, 366.

74. Jackson, *Bono's Politics*, 137–38; Emily Pierce, "Nussle Heeds Calls, Boosts AIDS Funds," *Roll Call*, June 1, 2004, www.rollcall.com/issues/49_130/-5700-1.html, accessed April 4, 2014.

75. Celia W. Dugger, "Rock Star Still Hasn't Found the African Aid He's Looking For," *New York Times*, May 15, 2007, www.nytimes.com/2007/05/15/world/africa/15bono.html?_r=1&oref=slogin, accessed April 7, 2014, cited in Kharas, "The New Reality of Aid," 53; Davis, "Feeding the World a Line?," 89–117; Bono, cited in Matthew Bishop, "Fighting Global Poverty: Who Will Be Relevant in 2020?," in Brainard and Chollet, *Global Development 2.0*, 49.

76. Bono, "Five Scenes, One Theme: A True If Unlikely Story," *New York Times*, November 15, 2009.

77. Brockington, *Celebrity Advocacy and International Development*, 121, 157.

78. Cited in Bono and Assayas, *Bono*, 364.

79. www.one.org/us/about, accessed February 9, 2015.

80. Lane, "Bill Gates and Bono."

81. Bono, "Transcript of Bono's Class Day Speech at Harvard," June 10, 2001, reproduced in *The U2 Reader: A Quarter Century of Commentary, Criticism, and Reviews*, ed. Hank Bordowitz (Milwaukee, WI: Hal Leonard, 2003), 153.

82. Bono and Assayas, *Bono*, 103.

83. Bono, "It's 2009. Do You Know Where Your Soul Is?," *New York Times*, April 18, 2009.

84. Bono, "Rebranding Africa," *New York Times*, July 10, 2009; Lane, "Bill Gates and Bono."

85. Bono, cited in Matthew Bishop, "Fighting Global Poverty," 48, 47.

86. Browne, *The Frontman*, 116.

87. Wall, *Bono*, 230; Jill Marino, "U2 Appear on Forbes Magazine's Highest Paid Musicians List," November 29, 2012, www.atu2.com/news/u2-appear-on-forbes-magazines-highest-paid-musicians-list.html, accessed April 11, 2014; Glenn Peoples, "Business Matters: Bono Will Make Maybe $10 Million, Not $1.5 Billion, from Facebook's IPO," *Billboard*, May 18, 2012, www.billboard.com/biz/articles/news/1096373/business-matters-bono-will-make-maybe-10-million-not-15-billion-from, accessed April 11, 2014.

88. Kay Bell, "U2's International Tax Avoidance: Good for Band's Bottom Line, Bad for Its and Bono's Reputation?," *Don't Mess with Taxes*, September 25, 2013, http://dontmesswithtaxes.typepad.com/dont_mess_with_taxes/2013/09/u2s-tax-avoidance-good-for-bands-bottom-line-bad-for-its-reputation.html, accessed April 14, 2014; Kathleen Caulderwood, "Bono, the $600M Net Worth Musician Whose U2 Band Is a Poster Child for Tax Avoidance, Slams Big Oil for Tax Avoidance," *International Business Times*, September 25, 2013,

www.ibtimes.com/bono-600m-net-worth-musician-whose-u2-band-poster-child-tax-avoidance-slams-big-oil-tax-avoidance, accessed April 14, 2014.

89. Bono and Assayas, *Bono*, 330.

90. Apart from a royalty for every U2 iPod sold. U2 and McCormick, *U2 by U2*, 330; "U2 Take on the World: Inside Rolling Stone's New Issue," *Rolling Stone*, October 23, 2014, www.rollingstone.com/music/news/u2-take-on-the-world-inside-rolling-stones-new-issue-20141023, accessed November 7, 2014; Niall Stokes, *U2: The Stories behind Every U2 Song* (London: Carlton, 2009), n.p.; Browne, *The Frontman*, 122.

91. Browne, *The Frontman*, 120, cited in Zeller, "Bono, Trying to Throw His Arms around the World."

92. Bono and Assayas, *Bono*, 332.

93. Bono and Assayas, *Bono*, 317.

94. Bono, *Bono*, 83–84.

95. "We're One, but We're Not the Same One," *The Irish Examiner*, March 11, 2009, www.irishexaminerusa.com/mt/2009/03/11/were_one_but_were_not_the_same.html, accessed April 11, 2014; Michael Brennan, "Burton Drags U2 into Corporate Tax Avoidance 'Scandal,'" *The Independent*, May 10, 2013, www.independent.ie/irish-news/burton-drags-u2-into-corporate-tax-avoidance-scandal-29255489.html, accessed April 11, 2014.

96. Cited in "McGuinness Opens Up on Zoo TV, the Netherlands Move and Much More," *Hot Press*, September 20, 2006, www.atu2.com/news/mcguinness-opens-up-on-zoo-tv-the-netherlands-move-and-much-more.html, accessed April 11, 2014.

97. Cited in Paul Gorman, "Paul McGuiness: How the Fifth Man Turned Empire Builder," reproduced in Bordowitz, *The U2 Reader*, 291.

98. Nick Cohen, "It Isn't Just Bono's U2 Who Are Talking through Their Hat about Tax Avoidance," *The Observer*, October 21, 2006, www.theguardian.com/commentisfree/2006/oct/22/comment.theobserver, accessed April 11, 2014; Monbiot, "Bono Can't Help Africans by Stealing Their Voice."

99. Browne, *The Frontman*, 38; Brennan, "Burton Drags U2 into Corporate Tax Avoidance 'Scandal.'"

100. Mary Anastasia O'Grady, "Bono Needs to Pay Up," *Wall Street Journal*, June 8, 2011, http://online.wsj.com/article/SB10001424052702304259304576373771000025408.html, accessed April 11, 2014; Sean Michaels, "U2 Accused of 'Robbing the World's Poor,'" *The Guardian*, February 27, 2009, www.guardian.co.uk/music/2009/feb/27/u2-irish-aid-group-coalition, accessed April 11, 2014, cited in Browne, *The Frontman*, 43.

101. Steve Stockman, *Walk On: The Spiritual Journey of U2* (Orlando, FL: Relevant Books, 2005), 172; Bell, "U2's International Tax Avoidance."

102. Cited in Browne, *The Frontman*, 39; Richard Osley, "Bono Defends U2's Tax Arrangement: We Are in 'Total Harmony' with Irish Government's Philosophy," *The Independent*, September 22, 2013, www.independent.co.uk/arts-entertainment/music/news/bono-defends-u2s-tax-arrangement-we-are-in-total-harmony-with-irish-governments-philosophy-8833065.html, accessed April 14, 2014.

103. Cited in Browne, *The Frontman*, 51; Stokes, "U2—An Outstanding Artistic Force."

104. Caulderwood, "Bono, the $600M Net Worth Musician Whose U2 Band Is a Poster Child for Tax Avoidance, Slams Big Oil for Tax Avoidance."

105. Bono and Assayas, *Bono*, 165.

CONCLUSION

1. Višnja Cogan, *U2: An Irish Phenomenon* (Cork: The Collins Press, 2006), 235.

2. Jay Cocks, "Band on the Run," reproduced in *The U2 Reader: A Quarter Century of Commentary, Criticism, and Reviews*, ed. Hank Bordowitz (Milwaukee, WI: Hal Leonard, 2003), 54.

3. *U2: The Ultimate Compendium of Interviews, Articles, Facts, and Opinions from the Files of* Rolling Stone (New York: Hyperion, 1994), 72, 77.

4. Liam Mackey, "Articulate Speech of the Heart," *Hot Press*, August 5, 1983, www.hotpress.com/archive/549220.html, accessed November 10, 2014.

5. Cited in Martha P. Trachtenberg, *Bono: Rock Star Activist* (Berkeley Heights, NJ: Enslow Publishers, 2008), 50.

6. Arthur E. Lizie, *Dreaming the World: U2 Fans, Online Community and Intellectual Communication* (Cresskill, NJ: Hampton Press, 2009), 175, 187.

7. Cogan, *U2*, 235.

8. Cited in Rachel E. Seiler, "Potent Crossroads: Where U2 and Progressive Awareness Meet," in *Exploring U2: Is This Rock 'n' Roll? Essays on the Music, Work, and Influence of U2*, ed. Scott Calhoun (Lanham, MD: Scarecrow Press, 2012), 39, 42.

9. Seiler, "Potent Crossroads," 43, 44.

10. Seiler, "Potent Crossroads," 45, 47.

11. www.gypsyheart.com.au/page10.htm, no longer active.

12. Mick Wall, *Bono: In the Name of Love* (New York: Thunder's Mouth Press, 2005), 17.

13. Bono, cited in Christian Scharen, *One Step Closer: Why U2 Matters to Those Seeking God* (Grand Rapids, MI: Brazos Press, 2006), 135.

14. Beth Maynard, "Where *Leitourgia* Has No Name: U2 Live," in Calhoun, *Exploring U2*, 159.

15. David Hajdu, "Forever Young? In Some Ways, Yes," *New York Times*, May 23, 2011, www.nytimes.com/2011/05/24/opinion/24hajdu.html, accessed December 2, 2014.

16. Seiler, "Potent Crossroads," 51.

17. Scott Calhoun also noticed this in "Across the Universe: U2's Hope in Space and Time," in *Exploring U2*, 245.

18. November 6, 2014.

19. John Waters, *Race of Angels: The Genesis of U2* (London: Fourth Estate, 1994), 67.

20. Calhoun, "Across the Universe," 245, 248.

21. Anthony DeCurtis, "Foreword: U2—Contents and Discontents," in Calhoun, *Exploring U2*, xviii.

BIBLIOGRAPHY

Alan, Carter. *U2: Wide Awake in America—12 Years with U2 Backstage and Beyond.* London: Boxtree, 1992.

Appiah, Kwame Anthony. *Cosmopolitanism: Ethics in a World of Strangers.* New York: Norton, 2006.

Atkinson, Nathalie. "Ali Hewson and Bono's Return to Edun." *National Post,* March 5, 2011.

Bailie, Stuart, and Hugh Lineham. "Saints or Sinners." *Irish Times,* July 18, 2008.

"Band Aid 30 Faces Criticism for Being Damaging to Africa." BBC, November 18, 2014.

Bedard, Paul. "Bono: George Bush, Evangelicals Saved 9 Million AIDS Victims." *Washington Examiner,* June 24, 2013.

Bell, Kay. "U2's International Tax Avoidance: Good for Band's Bottom Line, Bad for Its and Bono's Reputation?" *Don't Mess with Taxes,* September 25, 2013.

Block, Adam. "Pure Bono (Part 1)." *Mother Jones Magazine,* May 1, 1989.

Blow, Richard. "Bono Turns Up the Political Heat." *George Magazine,* April 1, 2000.

Bono. *Bono: In His Own Words.* New York: Omnibus Press, 1997.

Bono. *A String of Pearls: Photographs of Ethiopia.* N.p., 1988.

"Bono: 'I'm Tired of Just Dreaming.'" *Irish Independent,* March 2, 2002.

"Bono's Thin Ecclesiology." *Christianity Today,* March 1, 2003.

"Bono: Not Facing AIDS Crisis 'Foolhardy.'" Fox News, September 1, 2004.

Bono. "I Am a Witness. What Can I Do?" *The Independent,* May 16, 2006, 38.

Bono. "Message 2U." *Vanity Fair,* July 2007.

Bono. *On the Move: A Speech.* Nashville, TN: W. Publishing Group, 2007.

Bono. "It's 2009. Do You Know Where Your Soul Is?" *New York Times,* April 18, 2009.

Bono. "Rebranding Africa." *New York Times,* July 10, 2009.

Bono. "Five Scenes, One Theme: A True If Unlikely Story." *New York Times,* November 15, 2009.

Bono. "Africa Reboots." *New York Times,* April 17, 2010.

Bono. "In Ireland, Tuesday's Grace." *New York Times,* June 19, 2010.

Bono. "M.D.G.'s for Beginners . . . and Finishers." *New York Times,* September 18, 2010.

Bono and Michka Assayas. *Bono.* New York: Riverhead Books, 2005.

Bordowitz, Hank, ed. *The U2 Reader: A Quarter Century of Commentary, Criticism, and Reviews.* Milwaukee, WI: Hal Leonard, 2003.

Bowler, Dave, and Bryan Dray. *U2: A Conspiracy of Hope.* London: Sidgwick & Jackson, 1993.

Brainard, Lael, and Derek Chollet, eds. *Global Development 2.0: Can Philanthropists, the Public, and the Poor Make Poverty History?* Washington, DC: Brookings Institution Press, 2008.

Brennan, Michael. "Burton Drags U2 into Corporate Tax Avoidance 'Scandal.'" *The Independent*, May 10, 2013.
Brockington, Dan. *Celebrity Advocacy and International Development.* New York: Routledge, 2014.
Browne, Harry. *The Frontman: Bono (In the Name of Power).* London: Verso, 2013.
Busby, Joshua William. "Bono Made Jesse Helms Cry: Jubilee 2000, Debt Relief, and Moral Action in International Politics." *International Studies Quarterly* 51 (June 2007): 247–75.
Calhoun, Scott. "Where Could We Go from Here? The State of U2 Studies." *Books and Culture*, November/December 2009, 14–15.
———, ed. *Exploring U2: Is This Rock 'n' Roll? Essays on the Music, Work, and Influence of U2.* Lanham, MD: Scarecrow Press, 2012.
"Can Bono Save the Third World?" *The Daily Beast*, January 23, 2000.
Carr, David. "Citizen Bono Brings Africa to the Idle Rich." *New York Times*, March 5, 2007.
Catanzarite, Stephen. *Achtung Baby: Meditations on Love in the Shadow of the Fall.* New York: Continuum, 2007.
Caulderwood, Kathleen. "Bono, the $600M Net Worth Musician Whose U2 Band Is a Poster Child for Tax Avoidance, Slams Big Oil for Tax Avoidance." *International Business Times*, September 25, 2013.
Cerkez, Aida, and Sabina Niksic. "1993 Bosnian Beauty Queen Stood Up against War." Associated Press, April 4, 2012.
Cogan, Višnja. *U2: An Irish Phenomenon.* Cork: The Collins Press, 2006.
Cohen, Nick. "It Isn't Just Bono's U2 Who Are Talking through Their Hat about Tax Avoidance." *The Observer*, October 21, 2006.
Colgan, Ann-Louis. "Africa Policy Outlook 2005." *Foreign Policy in Focus*, October 3, 2005.
Collier, Paul. *The Bottom Billion: Why the Poorest Countries Are Failing and What Can Be Done about It.* New York: Oxford University Press, 2007.
Cooper, Andrew. "Beyond One Image Fits All: Bono and the Complexity of Celebrity Diplomacy." *Global Governance: A Review of Multilateralism and International Organizations* 14, no. 3 (July–September 2008): 265–72.
Cullather, Nick. *The Hungry World: America's Cold War Battle against Poverty in Asia.* Cambridge, MA: Harvard University Press, 2010.
Curiel, Jonathan. "Star Power: When Celebrities Support Causes, Who Really Winds Up Benefiting?" *SF Gate*, June 5, 2005.
Dart, John. "Bono: 'Juxtapositioning' for the World's Poor." *Christian Century*, February 13–20, 2002.
Davis, Louise. "Feeding the World a Line? Celebrity Activism and Ethical Consumer Practices from Live Aid to Product Red." *Nordic Journal of English Studies* 9, no. 3 (2010): 89–117.
DeCurtis, Anthony. "Bono: The Beliefnet Interview," February 2001. www.beliefnet.com/Entertainment/Music/2001/02/Bono-The-Beliefnet-Interview.aspx, accessed November 11, 2014.
———. "Bono's Crusade." *Rolling Stone*, March 6, 2002.
Dettmar, Kevin J. H., and William Richey, eds. *Reading Rock and Roll: Authenticity, Appropriation, Aesthetics.* New York: Columbia University Press, 1999.
Dingfelder, Sadie F. "Reflecting on Narcissism: Are Young People More Self-Obsessed Than Ever Before?" *Monitor on Psychology* 42, no. 2 (February 2011), 64.
Dirchfield, Christin. *Bono.* Ann Arbor, MI: Cherry Lake Publishing, 2008.
Dugger, Celia W. "Rock Star Still Hasn't Found the African Aid He's Looking For." *New York Times*, May 15, 2007.
Dunphy, Eamon. *Unforgettable Fire: The Story of U2.* London: Viking, 1987.
Easterly, William. *The Elusive Quest for Growth.* Cambridge, MA: MIT Press, 2001.
———. *The White Man's Burden.* New York: Penguin, 2007.
Eaton, Jenny, and Kate Etue, eds. *The aWAKE Project: United against the African AIDS Crisis.* Nashville, TN: W. Publishing Group, 2002.
"Electric Burma for Aung San Suu Kyi," June 18, 2012. http://www.u2.com/tour/article/title/electric-burma-for-aung-san-suu-kyi/news/36/112, accessed February 9, 2015.

Elliott, Larry, and David Teathe. "Blair Hails Push on Debt Relief for Poorest." *World Security Network*, June 11, 2004.

Essex, Andrew. "Unforgettable Fire: The Ongoing Beatification of Bono." *U2-Atomic-Articles*, October 22, 2001.

Everett, Walter, ed. *Expression in Pop-Rock Music.* New York: Routledge, 2000.

Fallon, B. P. *U2 Faraway So Close.* Boston: Little, Brown, 1994.

Falsani, Cathleen. "Bono's American Prayer." *Christianity Today*, March 1, 2003.

Fisher, William W., III, and Cyrill P. Rigamonti. "The South African AIDS Controversy: A Case Study in Patent Law and Policy." Harvard Law School, February 2005.

Flanagan, Bill. *U2 at the End of the World.* New York: Dell, 1995.

Frank, Robert H. *Luxury Fever: Money and Happiness in an Era of Excess.* Princeton, NJ: Princeton University Press, 1999.

Fricke, David. "U2 Dissect 'Bomb.'" *Rolling Stone*, December 15, 2004.

Fuse ODG. "Why I Had to Turn Down Band AID." *The Guardian*, November 19, 2014.

Gardner, Elysa. "Bono's Looking Back, and Ahead, and Within." *USA Today*, January 31, 2014, 7B.

Garrett, Greg. *We Get to Carry Each Other: The Gospel According to U2.* Louisville, KY: Westminster John Knox Press, 2009.

Geivett, R. Douglas, and James S. Spiegel, eds. *Faith, Film and Philosophy: Big Ideas on the Big Screen.* Downers Grove, IL: InterVarsity Press, 2007.

Gilmour, Michael, ed. *Call Me the Seeker: Listening to Religion in Popular Music.* New York: Continuum, 2005.

Greig, Alastair, David Hulme, and Mark Turner. *Challenging Global Inequality: Development Theory and Practice in the 21st Century.* New York: Palgrave Macmillan, 2007.

Hajdu, David. "Forever Young? In Some Ways, Yes." *New York Times*, May 23, 2011.

Hannerz, Ulf. "Cosmopolitans and Locals in World Culture." *Theory, Culture and Society* 7 (1990): 237–51.

Heim, David. "Breakfast with Bono." *Christian Century*, March 21, 2006.

Hendershot, Karen, and Jill Sperandio. "Study Abroad and Development of Global Citizen Identity and Cosmopolitan Ideals in Undergraduates." *Current Issues in Comparative Education* 12, no. 1 (2009): 45–55.

Henke, James. "The Edge: The Rolling Stone Interview." *Rolling Stone*, March 10, 1987.

Hertz, Noreena. *The Debt Threat: How Debt Is Destroying the Developing World.* New York: HarperCollins, 2004.

Hiatt, Brian. "Trying to Throw Their Arms around the World." *Rolling Stone*, November 6, 2014.

Hilburn, Robert. "U2: At Home in Dublin." *Los Angeles Times*, April 12, 1987.

Holm-Hudson, Kevin. "Et Tu, U2? 'Wake Up Dead Man' and Bono's Perceived Betrayal of the Faith." *Journal of Religion and Popular Culture* 16, no. 2 (2007): n.p.

Jackson, Laura. *Bono: His Life, Music, and Passions.* New York: Citadel Press, 2003.

Jackson, Nathan Dwayne. *Bono's Politics: The Future of Celebrity Political Activism.* Saarbrücken: VDM Verlag Dr. Müller, 2008.

Javers, Eamon. "Bono's K Street Connection." *CQ Weekly*, March 28, 2005, 762–63.

Karlberg, Michael. "Discourse, Identity, and Global Citizenship." *Peace Review* 20, no. 3 (2008): 310–20.

Karliner, Joshua. *The Corporate Planet: Ecology and Politics in the Age of Globalization.* San Francisco: Sierra Club Books, 1997.

Kearney, Richard, ed. *Across the Frontiers: Ireland in the 1990s—Cultural, Political, Economic.* Dublin: Wolfhound Press, 1989.

Kiviat, Barbara, and Bill Gates. "Making Capitalism More Creative." *Time*, July 31, 2008.

Kokkoris, Tassoula E. "Secrets of Sarajevo: 20 Years Later." *@U2*, April 26, 2013.

Kot, Greg. "Bono: 'We Need to Talk.'" *Chicago Tribune*, May 22, 2005.

Krauss, Clifford. "Canada's Leader Is a Skinflint, Says a Former Admirer, Bono." *New York Times*, May 4, 2005.

Lasch, Christopher. *The Culture of Narcissism.* New York: Norton, 1979.

Laurence, Jeremy. "Why RED Can Boost Global Fund and Its War on HIV." *The Independent*, May 16, 2006.

Light, Alan. "Band of the Year: Rock's Unbreakable Heart." *Spin*, January 1, 2002.

Lizie, Arthur E. *Dreaming the World: U2 Fans, Online Community and Intellectual Communication*. Cresskill, NJ: Hampton Press, 2009.

Lowry, Annie. "The Wealth Gap in America Is Growing, Too." *New York Times*, April 2, 2014.

Mackey, Liam. "Articulate Speech of the Heart." *Hot Press*, August 5, 1983.

Maddex, Bobby. "A God-Shaped Hole: Can U2 and a New Generation of Seekers Ever Fill It?" *Gadfly*, August 1997, n.p.

Malcolm, Lynne. "Research Says Young People Today Are More Narcissistic Than Ever." *All in the Mind*, May 16, 2014.

Masterson, John. "Ali's Other Eden." *Irish Independent*, March 8, 2005.

McFlicker, Todd. *All You Need Is Love to Dismantle an Atomic Bomb: How the Beatles and U2 Changed the World*. New York: Continuum, 2007.

McGee, Matt. *U2: A Diary*. London: Omnibus, 2008.

McGinty, Stephen. "Bono Still Hasn't Found What He Is Looking For: Debt Relief." *The Scotsman*, September 25, 2004.

"McGuinness Opens Up on Zoo TV, the Netherlands Move and Much More." *Hot Press*, September 20, 2006.

McLaughlin, Noel. "Bono! Do You Ever Take Those Wretched Sunglasses Off? U2 and the Performance of Irishness." *Popular Music History* 4, no. 3 (2009): 309–31.

Menkes, Suzy. "Philanthropy in Fashion." *New York Times*, November 15, 2012.

Michaels, Sean. "U2 Accused of 'Robbing the World's Poor.'" *The Guardian*, February 27, 2009.

Milanovic, Branko. *Worlds Apart: Measuring International and Global Inequality*. Princeton, NJ: Princeton University Press, 2005.

Monbiot, George. "Bono Can't Help Africans by Stealing Their Voice." *The Guardian*, June 17, 2013.

Moyo, Dambisa. *Dead Aid: Why Aid Is Not Working and How There Is a Better Way for Africa*. New York: Farrar, Straus and Giroux, 2009.

Nixon, Ron. "Bottom Line for (Red)." *New York Times*, February 6, 2008.

O'Brien, Chris. "'Factivist' Bono Projects Poverty Rate of Zero by 2030." *Los Angeles Times*, February 26, 2013.

O'Grady, Mary Anastasia. "Bono Needs to Pay Up." *Wall Street Journal*, June 8, 2011.

Osley, Richard. "Bono Defends U2's Tax Arrangement: We Are in 'Total Harmony' with Irish Government's Philosophy." *The Independent*, September 22, 2013.

Pallas, Christopher. "Identity, Individualism, and Activism beyond the State: Examining the Impacts of Global Citizenship." *Global Society: Journal of Interdisciplinary International Relations* 26, no. 2 (2012): 169–89.

Parkyn, Geoff. *U2: Touch the Flame*. New York: Perigree Books, 1988.

Pichler, Florian. "Cosmopolitanism in a Global Perspective: An International Comparison of Open-Minded Orientations and Identity in Relation to Globalization." *International Sociology* 27, no. 1 (2012): 21–50.

Pierce, Emily. "Nussle Heeds Calls, Boosts AIDS Funds." *Roll Call*, June 1, 2004.

Ponte, Stefano, Lisa Ann Richey, and Mike Baab. "Bono's Product (RED) Initiative: Corporate Social Responsibility That Solves the Problems of 'Distant Others.'" *Third World Quarterly* 30, no. 2 (2009): 305–6.

Povoledo, Elisabetta. "For Fashion's Glitterati, 'Trade Not Aid' Shoots through IHT Conference." *International Herald Tribune*, November 16, 2012.

Pulcini, Elena. *Care of the World: Fear, Responsibility, and Justice in the Global Age*. Translated by Karen Whittle. New York: Springer, 2013.

Putnam, Robert. *Bowling Alone: The Collapse and Revival of American Community*. New York: Simon & Schuster, 2000.

Quinn, Steven. "U2 and the Performance of (a Numb) Resistance." *Social Semiotics* 9, no. 1 (1999): 67–83.

Ramert, Lynn. "A Century Apart: The Personality Performances of Oscar Wilde in the 1890s and U2's Bono in the 1990s." *Popular Music and Society* 32, no. 4 (2009): 447–60.

Reiff, Mark R. *Exploitation and Economic Justice in the Liberal Capitalist State.* New York: Oxford University Press, 2013.

Richey, Lisa Ann, and Stefano Ponte. *Brand Aid: Shopping Well to Save the World.* Minneapolis: University of Minnesota Press, 2011.

Rothkopf, David. *Superclass: The Global Power Elite and the World They Are Making.* New York: Farrar, Straus and Giroux, 2008.

Ryzik, Melena. "Charlize Theron's Influence, Anderson Cooper's Help." *New York Times,* January 12, 2014.

Sachs, Jeffrey D. *The End of Poverty: Economic Possibilities for Our Time.* New York: Penguin, 2005.

———. *Common Wealth: Economics for a Crowded Planet.* New York: Penguin, 2008.

Sandel, Michael J. *What Money Can't Buy: The Moral Limits of Markets.* New York: Farrar, Straus and Giroux, 2012.

Savage, Mike, Gaynor Bagnall, and Brian Longhurst. *Globalization and Belonging.* London: Sage, 2005.

Scharen, Christian. *One Step Closer: Why U2 Matters to Those Seeking God.* Grand Rapids, MI: Brazos Press, 2006.

Seales, Chad E. "Burned over Bono: U2's Rock 'n' Roll Messiah and His Religious Politic." *Journal of Religion and Popular Culture* 14, no. 1 (2006): n.p.

Selections from the Book of Psalms, introduction by Bono. New York: Grove Press, 1999.

Sevcik, J. C. "The US Is Not a Democracy but an Oligarchy, Study Concludes." United Press International, April 16, 2014.

Sheffield, Rob. Review of "Music from 'Spider-Man: Turn Off the Dark.'" *Rolling Stone,* June 14, 2011.

Smyth, Gerry. *Space and the Irish Cultural Imagination.* New York: Palgrave, 2001.

Stallard, Michael. "3 Practices CEOs Should Adopt from This Rock Star." Fox Business, January 9, 2014.

"Stars Condemn G8 Violence." BBC News, July 22, 2001.

Stockman, Steve. *Walk On: The Spiritual Journey of U2.* Orlando, FL: Relevant Books, 2005.

Stokes, Niall, ed. *The U2 File: A Hot Press U2 History, 1978–1985.* London: Omnibus, 1985.

———, ed. *U2: Three Chords and the Truth.* New York: Harmony Books, 1989.

———. "Matter of Life and Death—Part 1." *Hot Press Annual 2002,* December 1, 2001.

———. *U2: The Stories behind Every U2 Song.* London: Carlton, 2009.

———. "U2—An Outstanding Artistic Force." *Hot Press,* October 30, 2014.

"Stop the Madness." Interview with Rupert Cornwell. *Globe and Mail,* July 6, 2002.

Street, John. "Bob, Bono and Tony B: The Popular Artist as Politician." *Media, Culture and Society* 24 (2002): 433–41.

Tangonyire, Raymond Chegedua, SJ, and Lawrence Kyaligonza Achal, SJ. *Economic Behaviour As If Others Too Had Interests.* Bamenda, Cameroon: Langaa RPCIG, 2012.

Taylor, Charles. *The Ethics of Authenticity.* Cambridge, MA: Harvard University Press, 1992.

Trachtenberg, Martha P. *Bono: Rock Star Activist.* Berkeley Heights, NJ: Enslow Publishers, 2008.

"Transcript: Bono Remarks at the National Prayer Breakfast." *USA Today,* February 2, 2006.

Traub, James. "The Statesman." *New York Times Magazine,* September 18, 2005, 80+.

———. "The Celebrity Solution." *New York Times,* March 9, 2008.

Tsaliki, Liza, Christos A. Frangonikolopoulos, and Asteris Huliaras, eds. *Transnational Celebrity Activism in Global Politics: Changing the World?* Chicago: Intellect, 2011.

Twenge, Jean M., and W. Keith Campbell. *The Narcissism Epidemic: Living in the Age of Entitlement.* New York: Atria, 2009.

Tyrangiel, Josh. "Music: Bono." *Time,* March 4, 2002.

U2: The Ultimate Compendium of Interviews, Articles, Facts, and Opinions from the Files of Rolling Stone. New York: Hyperion, 1994.

U2: The Best of Propaganda: 20 Years of the Official U2 Magazine. New York: Thunder's Mouth Press, 2003.

U2 and Neil McCormick. *U2 by U2*. New York: HarperCollins, 2006.

"U2 Speak of Their 'Long History' with Mandela." *RTÉ*, November 26, 2013.

Vagacs, Robert. *Religious Nuts, Political Fanatics: U2 in Theological Perspective*. Eugene, OR: Cascade Books, 2005.

Wall, Mick. *Bono: In the Name of Love*. New York: Thunder's Mouth Press, 2005.

Washburn, Kim. *Breaking Through by Grace: The Bono Story*. Grand Rapids, MI: Zonderkidz, 2010.

Waters, John. *Race of Angels: The Genesis of U2*. London: Fourth Estate, 1994.

Wenner, Jann S. "Bono: The Rolling Stone Interview." *Rolling Stone*, November 3, 2005.

"We're One, But We're Not the Same One," *The Irish Examiner,* March 11, 2009.

Whiteley, Raewynne J., and Beth Maynard, eds. *Get Up Off Your Knees: Preaching the U2 Catalog*. Cambridge, MA: Cowley Publications, 2003.

Wrathall, Mark, ed. *U2 and Philosophy: How to Decipher an Atomic Band*. Chicago: Open Court, 2006.

Zeleny, Jeff. "The 2008 Campaign: Bono's Poverty-Fighting Plan Promoted by Two Ex-Senators." *New York Times*, June 12, 2007.

Zeller, Tom, Jr. "Bono, Trying to Throw His Arms around the World." *New York Times*, November 13, 2006.

INDEX

ABOUT THE AUTHOR

Alan McPherson is a historian of international relations. He is professor of international and area studies, ConocoPhillips chair in Latin American studies, and director of the Center for the Americas at the University of Oklahoma. He holds degrees from the University of Montreal and San Francisco State University as well as a PhD in history from the University of North Carolina at Chapel Hill.

Dr. McPherson wrote the prize-winning books *Yankee No! Anti-Americanism in U.S.-Latin American Relations* (2003) and *The Invaded: How Latin Americans and Their Allies Fought and Ended U.S. Occupations* (2014), as well as *Intimate Ties, Bitter Struggles: The United States and Latin America since 1945* (2006). He also edited *Anti-Americanism in Latin America and the Caribbean* (2006) and the *Encyclopedia of U.S. Interventions in Latin America* (2013) and coedited *The Anti-American Century* (2007). He has also published journal articles, book chapters, and op-eds.

He has been a fellow at Harvard University and twice a Fulbright Fellow in the Dominican Republic and Argentina.

Dr. McPherson has been a fan of U2's music and activism since 1984. The band solidified his early interest in Latin America and his leadership of an Amnesty International chapter. He lives in Norman, Oklahoma.

More information on Dr. McPherson can be found at www.ou.edu/content/cis/ias/faculty/alan-mcpherson.html.